Praise for *The Homeschool [Advantage]*

"As a Type-A box checker, I have struggled to embrace the unique benefits of homeschooling. Colleen Kessler has been the mentor who inspired me to understand that I can best serve my kids by embracing those benefits instead of staying stuck in a public school paradigm. With *The Homeschool Advantage*, she will inspire you, too."

—Pam Barnhill,
Host of the Homeschool Better Together Podcast

"*The Homeschool Advantage* is a must-read for any parent considering or currently homeschooling. It stands out not just as a guide, but also as a source of encouragement. Discover and be reminded of the profound impact parents can have when they step into the driver's seat of their children's education. This book is both a memoir and a manifesto from Colleen Kessler for her love of teaching but subsequent disillusionment with the education system. This book is a one-size-fits-all approach to education, and highlights the significant advantages of homeschooling in fostering a child's unique abilities and interests. Empowering, enlightening, entertaining, and so much more!"

—Dennis Dinoia,
M.Ed., Mr. D Math

"Colleen Kessler shares from the depth of her experience as a long-term homeschool parent, a mother of differently wired kids, and a recognized authority on gifted studies. In *The Homeschool Advantage*, she strengthens our resolve and self-trust as homeschooling parents, reminding us that home education is not just one alternative for our kids' learning, but that it may, in fact, be the best option of all!"

—Jamie C. Martin,
Veteran Homeschool Parent, Editor of SimpleHomeschool.net and
Bestselling Author of Give Your Child the World

"Many people support homeschooling or recommend certain methods of homeschooling, and that's all fine, but Colleen Kessler is a passionate advocate for homeschoolers. She is in the trenches, fighting for the real families and their always-unique kids. She pairs energetic advocacy with a bright mind alive with inspiring ideas and a generous heart to serve. Uncertain, worried, and overwhelmed families are desperate for a champion like Colleen Kessler."

—S.D. Smith,
Author of The Green Ember Series

"Colleen combines her passion for homeschooling with her real-life experiences to share the value and benefits of homeschooling. Whether you are thinking of homeschooling or need a reminder of why you chose to homeschool in the first place, this book will encourage you and share practical insight into the beauty of homeschooling."

"Colleen Kessler delivers such a rock-solid blueprint for why homeschooling better aligns with how our kids learn and what they need to succeed that you'll never even be tempted to place your kids in the system again. This book is a must-read for all homeschooling parents, offering practical steps for immediate action and profound insights that will forever transform your ideas about education. After delving into these pages, you will be profoundly thankful because you will witness firsthand how embracing homeschooling truly grants your children *The Homeschool Advantage*."

"This book is a support for any homeschooling parent. Through Kessler's experiences and other parents' stories, it reminds us how to build up our kids, set up their environment, and choose the best adventures."

"In *The Homeschool Advantage*, Colleen Kessler masterfully captures the holistic nature of education—academically, emotionally, and socially—while highlighting the significance of following your child's interests and strengths. With her insightful guidance, you'll feel equipped to embrace your child's unique path, making this book an absolute must-have for any homeschooling family."

"Colleen Kessler combines a passion for homeschooling with real-life experience and research. *The Homeschool Advantage* is filled with actionable tips you can implement right away, plus mindset shifts that will bring long-term improvement to family life. Colleen encourages us that we really are the best teachers for our kids, and reminds us that we have the freedom to pursue what works best for our own unique families. I especially love her encouragement to prioritize adventure, connection, love, and listening in our homeschool life. If you need fresh inspiration or if you need a reminder that you CAN do this homeschool thing (and do it well), you won't want to miss this book!"

The Homeschool Advantage

The Homeschool Advantage

A Child-Focused Approach to Raising Lifelong Learners

Colleen Kessler, M.Ed.

JB JOSSEY-BASS™
A Wiley Brand

Photography:
Pages 111, 159: Colleen Kessler | Instagram: @colleenkessler
Pages 129, 132, 186, 199: Katie Krupa | Instagram: @katiekrupacreative
Pages 20, 90, 107, Author Headshot: Trevor Kessler | Instagram: @trevorjkessler
All Other Photos: Heather Tully | Instagram: @heathertullyphotography

Illustrations:
Pages 117, 118: Colleen Kessler | Instagram: @colleenkessler

Published by John Wiley & Sons, Inc., Hoboken, New Jersey.
Published simultaneously in Canada.

ISBNs: 9781394205738 (Paperback), 9781394205769 (ePDF), 9781394205752 (ePub)

For general information on our other products and services or for technical support, please contact
our Customer Care Department within the United States at (800) 762-2974, outside the United
States at (317) 572-3993 or fax (317) 572-4002.

Wiley also publishes its books in a variety of electronic formats. Some content that appears in print
may not be available in electronic formats. For more information about Wiley products, visit our
web site at www.wiley.com.

Library of Congress Control Number

LCCN 2024007588 (print) | LCCN 2024007589 (ebook)

Cover design: Paul McCarthy
Cover Art: © Getty Images/D3sign

SKY10077114_061124

To Brian — you inspire me to love.

To Trevor, Molly, Logan, and Isaac — you inspire me to learn every day.

To all the homeschool families I've met near and far — you inspire me through all you do to encourage your children to find out who they're meant to be.

In Loving Memory

Leonard Anthony Kessler (1941–2019)

To Grandpa Lenny — You were one of our biggest homeschool cheerleaders, and I'm grateful that our kids had the gift of so much time with you simply because they were home during the school day and could spend it learning and loving alongside you. You are loved and missed.

Contents

Acknowledgments

The future looks bright because of all you parents taking on the education of your own. You're raising the leaders, innovators, creators, and parents of tomorrow. Thank you for making the world a better place. Together, we can raise a strong generation that is resilient, kind, and ready to nurture and love one another and continue to learn for the love of it.

To all the people I have had the opportunity to learn from, coach, speak for, and get to know from around the world, I want to say thank you for being the inspiration and foundation for this book. It wouldn't exist without you.

Having an idea and turning it into a book is as challenging as it sounds. The experience is both difficult and rewarding. I especially want to thank the people who helped make this happen. Thank you to the team at Wiley and Jossey Bass for the opportunity to tackle this important project and bring it into the world so beautifully. The back and forth of hammering out ideas, details, and focus can be difficult, and I'm grateful I had the chance to have the guidance of Sam Ofman, Navin Vijayakumar, and Tracy Brown Hamilton, whose encouragement, support, and commitment to producing the best book possible was so appreciated. Thank you, also, to the design team and production staff for your tireless work in bringing a book to life that I'm excited to share with the world.

My poor, underfed, ignored children were subjected to the words, "You're on your own for dinner tonight. Pretend I'm not home. I need to work on my book," so many times Isaac told me he "can't wait until it's done. I miss you." Thank you for eating endless meals of instant oatmeal, frozen mac and cheese, ramen, and sandwiches. I promise I'll cook for you again soon.

I couldn't possibly do any of the work I do without the best, smartest, strongest, and most supportive husband ever. This book was written during some of our busiest months ever. You think that parenting toddlers is crazy, but the teen years are an exercise in triangulating schedules, mapping out routes, and waiting in parking lots for endlessly long hours while they have fun, but don't want you around. Throughout it all, Brian, you were a rock — exactly the foundation I and the kids needed to hold on and be strong ourselves. I've never loved you more than I do right now. Thank you for always believing in me.

I have so many amazing friends, colleagues, and cheerleaders that I can't possibly mention them all, but there are a handful who have shared stories of their homeschooling and have given me so much support through this process and put up with hearing about the book again and again and again. Thank you to Cheryl Pitt and Aurie Good — I honestly don't know what I'd do without you two in my life. Thank goodness for Voxer! Cindy West, you are one of the best humans I know. Thank you for always being there for me. You make my life richer. Shawna Wingert, thank you for encouraging me at the start of all of this. You're a huge reason this book is in the world today. And thank you to all of the people who have helped bring kids to rehearsals and practices and dinners and parties while I was locked up in my office, chained to my desk. Thanks to the directors and teachers at The Aurora School of Music and The Fine Arts Association who opened up empty classrooms and spaces so I could work while my kids rehearsed. And to our homeschooling friends near and far . . . I love you all so very much.

About the Author

Colleen Kessler believes that you are the absolute best parent and teacher there is for your own children, no matter how their brains are wired.

The author of more than a dozen books for parents, teachers, and children; award-winning educator, educational coach, and consultant; international speaker; and passionate advocate for the needs of differently wired kids, Colleen has a B.S. in Elementary Education, an M.Ed. in Gifted Studies, and is the founder of the popular podcast and website *Raising Lifelong Learners* as well as The Learner's Lab – a community for homeschooling parents and their bright, quirky, outside-the-box kiddos.

Recent titles include *Raising Resilient Sons: A Boy Mom's Guide to Building a Strong, Confident, and Emotionally Intelligent Family*; *100 Backyard Activities That Are the Coolest, Dirtiest, Creepy-Crawliest Ever!*; *Raising Creative Kids: A Collection of Creativity Prompts for Children*; and *The Anxiety Toolkit: 96 Ways to Help Your Child Calm Their Worries*.

Colleen lives in northeast Ohio with her reading specialist husband, four delightfully differently wired kiddos, her lazy Pug, chaotic Border Collie, a dozen and a half chickens, two red-eared sliders, a bearded dragon, and an ever-changing assortment of small animals and insects. You can find her online at RaisingLifelongLearners.com.

Author's Note

Many clients, children, adults, friends, and listeners have shared their stories, experiences, and thoughts with me at conferences via voicemail, in calls, and online. I am so grateful for their generosity, bravery, and compassion. These are the heroes of the homeschooling culture – moms, dads, and kids in the trenches, learning and loving together. All names have been changed to preserve privacy.

You'll find quotes from homeschooling kids throughout the book in pull-out sections identified as "The Best Thing . . ." These were so fun to collect from friends, clients, and listeners! I asked parents to either ask their kids the question, "What is the BEST thing about homeschooling?" or "What do you like about homeschooling?" and their answers are just what you need to keep yourself motivated through the adventure of learning alongside your kiddos at home, so make sure you take time to read those!

I've also included stories of my own parenting, homeschooling, and family life. My four children and the stories they've agreed to allow me to share – they're *their* stories, after all – are sprinkled throughout the book. I remember being at a speaking event once with two of my kids, when one told me it was a little weird that some of the people she met talked to her as if they knew her well, and shared a story or anecdote they'd heard about that kiddo's life. I told her that her stories were hers, and she had a few choices if she felt weird about those attendees connecting with her like they knew her.

Since she and her siblings already have a say about which stories I tell when I speak to an audience or write a book, this was about her traveling with me. I told her she could a) choose not to travel to events with me anymore while I continued to tell her stories, b) continue to travel with me and I'd stop telling anecdotes about her when I spoke, or c) we'd keep things as they were and she'd work to regulate her reactions and emotions when someone came up to speak to her. She thought about it for a few days, then told me I needed to continue sharing so those parents who felt the need to connect with her over a story that touched them could know they weren't alone in their parenting and homeschooling, and that she wanted to continue to be a part of those moments.

Because my kids have seen the power of sharing and connecting with others, they agree to let me share their names and stories when I write and speak, so you'll hear a lot about them within the pages of this book, and I'll use their real names. I have four kiddos. At the time of this book's publication, Trevor is twenty-one and a homeschool graduate who began homeschooling in the middle of his first grade year, and is now working in the field of audio and video editing and production. He edits several podcasts (including mine) and shoots videos for online course creators, various freelance clients in multiple industries, and has an ongoing media contract with a racecar company.

Molly is currently seventeen, a high school senior who has homeschooled since the beginning, and plans on pursuing a BFA in musical theater once she graduates.

My daughter Logan is a fifteen-year-old high school freshman who loves animals and hopes to either become a zookeeper or an animal trainer.

And my youngest is eleven-year-old Isaac, who, at the time of this book's publication, doesn't know what he wants to do with his life as he is "just too young to make lifelong decisions because there's so much cool stuff to explore, Mom." So, if you see references to Trevor, Molly, Logan, or Isaac, they're not only my children, but four of the coolest, most interesting people I know.

For more homeschooling support, visit http://www.homeschooladvantage .info/ — created especially as a companion to this book or https://RaisingLife longLearners.com. You'll find articles, printables, links, resources, booklists, and ideas to enrich your homeschool, along with a contact page with a link to my email and voicemail so you can reach out if you ever need support. You are not alone in the homeschooling journey. Remember that.

Foreword

Homeschooling is funny business. We're all motivated to start homeschooling by different personal reasons, of course, but regardless of how you got here – to this moment in which you're reading a book about homeschooling – I can bet that at some point along the way you've had this thought: *Maybe my child will be better served if we educate at home?*

And then exactly 1.3 seconds later, you found yourself plagued by doubt. *Am I cut out for homeschooling? What if I can't give my child what they need? What if I'm bad at it? What if they hate it? What if they don't learn? What if I can't teach them? Have I completely lost my mind?*

In all the years of homeschooling my own six kids and in talking with thousands of homeschooling families all over the world, I have become convinced of this: **there are as many successful ways to homeschool as there are homeschooled kids**.

Successful homeschoolers use all different teaching methods – classical, nature-based, literature-based, STEM, unit studies, online, unschooling, or some combination of any of those or a million others. They follow very rigid schedules, no schedule at all, or something in between. They outsource everything, outsource nothing, or outsource a little. They homeschool with fancy science equipment, road school across the country, run homesteads, or (like me) none of the above. My own homeschool looks pretty ordinary, aside from our embarrassingly extensive library use.

Regardless of the myriad ways in which they do it, homeschooling families all over the world are raising confident, capable, well-educated kids.

And yet there is one thing that *all* homeschooling parents need, regardless of how they do it. **Every homeschooling parent needs someone in their corner.**

I have known the author of this book for a long time, and here is what I know: Colleen is in your corner. She's in mine, too.

By the end of this book, she'll give you the strong conviction that you are never alone, the confidence that you are the best teacher for your unique kids, and a wellspring of actionable ideas that will improve your home-school *today*.

In the pages of this book, you'll gain an awareness of your kids' strengths, a respect for the way they learn, and a plan for bringing those elements together so that your kids grow into the kind, capable, compassionate, and creative people you know them to be.

This is a book for parents who want to be their children's champion of home education. And that's just another way to say: this book is for you.

—Sarah Mackenzie
Author of *Teaching from Rest* and *The Read-Aloud Family*

Introduction

*When children are surrounded by curious and creative adults, they have
their own inner genius sparked into action.*

—Thomas Armstrong

*Just because a lot of people are saying the same thing loudly over and over,
doesn't mean it's true.*

—From *The Very Persistent Gappers of Frip* by
George Saunders

"He is an *extreme* thinker."

My son's pre-kindergarten teacher had invited me into the classroom
that day to observe him in the classroom setting, and so we could talk about
what the best options would be as he left the flexible learning environment
he was in for the more structured one he'd find at the local public school
he'd attend in kindergarten. She asked me to sit in the back of the room
and simply observe their read-aloud session and told me we'd talk afterward,
once she'd led the kids down the hall to their music class.

So I did.

I sat at a tiny chair in the back of the small classroom and watched as
she called the twelve kiddos over to the carpet to sit in a semicircle around
her chair. She pulled out a sweet picture book that featured a little boy
getting into all sorts of mischief during the day as he avoided what he was
supposed to be doing in the first place, only to realize what he'd done, then

backtrack to fix it all and complete the tasks before his mother returned home. Eleven of the kids in the class sat with rapt attention as the perky preschool teacher's voice filled the room.

Unlike the rest of his classmates, my son rolled around the side of the classroom. He crawled back and forth and back and forth. He sprawled on the table, then under the table. Just as he upended himself into a headstand against the wall, head cushioned by a pillow, and I was about to rise and intervene through my haze of first-time–mom mortification, the teacher caught my eye and shook her head gently. I sat through the rest of the story, while eleven little faces stared intently at the book in their teacher's hands and one closed his eyes while standing inverted against the side wall of the classroom, and felt like a complete failure.

Sure, he was my first child, and we all fail a bit with the firstborn, right? But I was also a teacher of almost fifteen years with a master's degree, an educational speaker and trainer, an author, and had nannied all through college. I wasn't inexperienced. And I knew this kid. He loved learning, and was always trying new things, seeking out people to learn from, hanging around the adults at parties so he could pump them about their jobs, interests, hobbies, and the books they were reading.

He should have been loving this read aloud.

And then the teacher started asking questions about the story to gauge comprehension and help the kiddos learn to talk about books. She asked the simple questions you'd expect in a classroom of five-year-olds: What color shirt was he wearing? Who was the story about? What happened at the end of the story? Where did it take place? Then she asked what the kids would have done if they'd been in the boy's place, and my son flipped out of his inversion and crept closer to the carpet. A few of the kiddos answered, saying they'd have done what the boy did, or hidden from the old man, or kept the pie all to themself.

My son raised his hand, "Mrs. Mowry, that boy had a lot of adventures, but if I were him, I would have just done what my mom asked me to do in the first place. He ended up having to fix a lot of messes and mistakes, and then still did what he was supposed to in the end. If he had just done it right away, he would have been able to play after and wouldn't have had so much extra work to deal with." When she asked if he always did what he was told right away he answered, with a sheepish grin in my direction, that, no, he didn't, and it did get him into trouble sometimes, but he usually wished he just done it right the first time and the boy should too.

His teacher sent a little smile in my direction, bustled the kids into line, and led them to the music teacher's room down the hall before coming back to talk to me. When she came back, she said those words to me and went on to tell me she was worried for his future in school. He was slated to attend our local public school the next year, and would be in a classroom of thirty or more students with teachers who were doing their best to meet the needs of all the kids in the rooms, but who just couldn't logistically be all to every one of the children in their classes.

Mrs. Mowry was an exemplary teacher. She took the time to get to know each of those little people in her tiny classroom – their strengths, weaknesses, interests, even the things they loathed – and met them where they were, encouraging them to learn and discover new things every day. For kids like my son, she incorporated movement, novelty, opportunities for higher-level thinking, and engaged him in interesting conversations as often as she could.

It was the best kind of educational experience – individualized to each of the kiddos in that room. At that moment in time, my son loved learning.

That love of learning began fading once he moved onto the local school for kindergarten. That transition marked the beginning of meetings, observations, parent-teacher conferences, failures, and disappointments. The first time we were called to come in and talk to the teacher was about him shredding his nap mat during the state-mandated *rest time*. His teacher, a kind and loving woman, was at wit's end because she was required by district policy to keep the kids on their nap mats for forty-five minutes each day and my son would roll, talk, disrupt, and shred the whole time.

After many conversations and conferences with guidance counselors and the principal, we finally reached a compromise. My son, who had given up naps for good at around six months of age, could have a small box of logic puzzles, games, and books at his rest spot, and he'd work on those silently on his mat for the required time, then he and his teacher would have a five-minute conversation about all the thoughts that had swirled in his head while he *rested* and couldn't talk about them.

But that wasn't the end of it.

We got to know the staff at the elementary school very well as we were repeatedly called in to discuss my son's behaviors. And they weren't the typical calls one expects when dealing with a rambunctious, impulsive boy forced to sit still for large chunks of his day. I'll never forget the day we were called into the guidance counselor's office because my son had allegedly threatened another boy on the playground and was being sent home and suspended the next day.

I saw his wide eyes staring out from across the hall where he sat with an aide while I was ushered into the office to talk with the guidance counselor, teacher, and principal. It seems that a playground volunteer had overheard him shout "I'm going to stab you with my knife," to his best friend, while they were playing a game of *Hunt*, one they'd invented while running the neighborhood, and played nearly every day after school. His friend laughed it off and shouted back that he'd never be caught, but the damage was done. While his buddy looked on in mild horror and tried to explain that it wasn't a big deal, the aide tugged my son inside to have the *threat* dealt with. And as the principal and guidance counselor calmly explained, the school had a zero-tolerance policy with regards to threatening language, so my six-year-old must be suspended.

While I agreed completely that my kiddo needed to understand that words have power, there were places and situations where certain words and games were inappropriate, and it was important to know how to behave in a school setting, I also didn't believe that zero-tolerance equaled zero-common-sense. When his principal suggested that the suspension was the only logical consequence, and that he'd have to also miss the *Dad's Day* event that was happening later that week despite my husband having already requested the day off, I protested.

That extreme thinker could learn a powerful lesson, but I was worried that this particular sentence would teach the wrong one, as the punishment didn't quite fit the crime. I suggested lost or heavily supervised recess time, even volunteering to come in myself and facilitate the most boring, miserable period so he'd want to behave and regain the joy of free play at recess, while making sure to guard his words going forward.

But the staff was immovable. Suspension was the only option, and the consequence would increase with any more infractions.

I told them I still felt they were missing out on an opportunity to teach him something about the power of words, as well as how to get along with others, but reassured that when I left the room, I'd support their decision within his hearing. I was worried, though, as I thought the wrong lesson may have been taught. My son was an outside-the-box thinker and processed the world in unique ways.

My worry was founded a few weeks later.

The school was preparing for standardized testing and my son showed open hostility about the idea of sitting still, filling in bubbles, and wasting – in his words – a whole day of learning fun. He loved his kindergarten teacher and the double room she shared with another teacher. They had set up a collaborative system where the kids moved freely between rooms, working in small groups, centers, and on projects throughout the day. It was the perfect setup for a kinesthetic mover like my guy was. And, now that the rest time problem had been solved, he loved being in the classroom.

However, he was dreading testing week.

The day before testing was to start, I received another call from the school, asking that I come in as soon as possible to meet with the principal. I dropped the baby and preschooler off at a neighbor's and rushed into the school. What was it now? The secretary was cryptic, though she assured me nobody was hurt.

I'll never forget seeing the principal's face as I sat across from her that day. She sat, waiting, and tapping her feet, at the table in the conference room. I remember her taking a deep breath and squaring her shoulders before speaking. She apologized for not thinking past a policy and remembering to take young kids' differences into account when we last met. It seems that, before she went into administration, she had worked with gifted elementary students and had forgotten to remember how quirky and innovative their thinking could be. And while my son was not yet identified as gifted, he was certainly like the kids she had once taught.

She told me that my son had set up things so that he and his best friend were talking next to the kid in the class who enjoyed a reputation as the class snitch during a break when an aide was facilitating the group. He told his buddy that he wanted to kill him. His friend told him to stop saying stupid things like that or he'd just get into trouble again and walked away.

The other kiddo, though, went right to that aide and told her what he'd said. She brought him to the principal's office and sat with him while they discussed calling me. The principal told my son that he'd earned another day's suspension, and she was disappointed that he hadn't learned how important words were when talking to other kids at school.

The principal, after taking that deep breath, told me that my son had leaned over her desk, looked her straight in the eyes, and calmly said, "Mrs. J., don't you think a threat of that magnitude deserves an entire week's suspension?" It seems that he'd staged the whole thing so he could get out of testing the next week.

Yes, my son *was* an extreme thinker, and despite us trying to fit that big, active, and often calculating mind into the system my husband and I had both made careers supporting, it just wasn't working out. Not only were behaviors escalating as he found the challenge of getting out of work much more interesting to figure out than the work itself, but his love of learning was crumbling before our eyes.

I'd love to tell you that the call to the principal's office over the testing week episode was the catalyst that sent us diving headfirst into homeschooling, but we weren't there yet. Homeschooling wasn't something I'd ever really considered back then. In fact, it took us until February of his first-grade year, and many, many phone calls, behavior challenges, and tests before we'd make the decision that changed our lives, and gave our children the advantage of a life filled with adventure, rabbit trails, nontraditional daily schedules, and an eclectic, interest-led, strengths-based approach that validated all I'd learned about best practice education in my graduate school classes, research, and time working with kids and their parents in and out of schools.

You picked up this book because you know homeschooling works and want to follow a different approach. You're not looking to re-create school-at-home. The school model isn't working for you — whether your kiddo has already been enrolled in school for a time or has never stepped foot inside a school building. You're ready for a child-focused approach that will instill a lifelong love of learning in your kids and bring your family closer together. This is the book for you.

Have you ever been frustrated when you have taken the time to read a book about a topic you know you love and want to learn more about doing, only to find that most of its content is spent convincing the reader why they should love the topic and want to do it? Then, only the last third or so has any suggestions for applying strategies to your life?

I've read many, many homeschooling books over the years that spell out very compelling reasons for taking on the enormous responsibility of teaching your own children at home. I share some of my favorites in the "Additional Resources" section of this book and on https://Homeschool Advantage.Resources – created especially as a companion to this book and on my website https://RaisingLifelongLearners.com. You'll find articles, printables, links, resources, booklists, and ideas to enrich your homeschool, along with a contact page with a link to my email and voicemail so you can reach out if you ever need support. When I began speaking at home-schooling conventions and conferences, I made a commitment to myself and anyone who would take their time to come to one of my sessions that the majority of my talks would be actionable suggestions they could use to improve their homeschool immediately, highlighted through storytell-ing and anecdotes to reassure them that they're not alone in anything they experience in the day to day of homeschooling.

I make that same promise to you as you read this book.

Whether you homeschool already or are curious about homeschool-ing or other alternative styles of learning, know that you are the best teacher for your kids. You can trust yourself *and* your children while embracing the adventure a lifestyle of learning for its own sake is, and the wonder it brings.

The wonderful thing about homeschooling is that parents aren't tied to one way of doing things. You're free to make it personal and tailor it to your family's needs and preferences. You can change it up week by week, month by month, or year by year. Because it means so much, homeschooling par-ents, you often doubt, feel like you're not doing enough or worry you're failing your kids in some way. This very worry, though, is what ensures you're giving your kids exactly what they need. Because you worry; you won't fail.

I want you to know that there IS a way to meet your kids right where they are, and build them up to be confident, resilient, and mentally healthy kids who are following their dreams and passions along the way to becom-ing the incredible adults they're meant to be. Too many of you scroll through your social media feeds on a rough day – and we *all* have them – and com-pare yourselves to the highlight reels others show.

You're left wallowing in doubt, worried that your kids won't ever be like "the kids of the parents you see online." But those families online have bad days, too. Every time I post about a rough day, a temper tantrum thrown, an abandoned unit study, or putting on a movie marathon and calling it school, I get hundreds of likes, comments, and DMs communicating some variation of, "I needed this today."

All those years ago, when we brought Trevor home from school, we figured we'd take it kid by kid and year by year, maybe putting one or more back into the school system one day. But we didn't. Trevor may have been the reason we started homeschooling, but we've kept on going for more than fifteen years so far because it works. And it's an incredible gift to be home with these really interesting little people, watching them grow into the amazing humans they're meant to be. When we started homeschooling, Trevor was in first grade, our daughter Molly was three, and my daughter Logan was a baby. Isaac wasn't even born yet. Here we are, years later, with a graduate, two high schoolers, and one on the verge of middle school. The younger three kids have never gone to school and will graduate from our homeschool like their big brother. You'll read more about them in the coming chapters.

They are thriving.

Your kiddos can, too.

Remember, you're meeting your kids' needs every day in teeny, tiny ways and big, huge ways, so be encouraged. Know you can not only make it homeschooling your kids through high school, but you, too, can thrive while doing it. You can enjoy the process of learning alongside your kids, the rabbit trails you follow because you didn't know every answer to every question, and the adventure of discovering wonder through the eyes of your little ones *and* your teens. And you can do all this in a way that lights your unique family up, taps into your individual and collective strengths, and leads your kids to follow interests and passions.

Let's do this together.

1 | Why Homeschool?

I suppose it is because nearly all children go to school nowadays and have things arranged for them that they seem so forlornly unable to produce their own ideas.

—Agatha Christie

Believe something and the Universe is on its way to being changed. Because you've changed, by believing. Once you've changed, other things start to follow. Isn't that the way it works?
—From *So You Want to Be a Wizard* by Diane Dune

Growing up, I loved school. I was good at it. A people-pleaser from the start who lived in a home where the adults vacillated between impossible to please or downright indifferent, I knew I could count on school to be the place where my efforts were validated and appreciated. I became friends with several teachers, babysitting for their children, participating in the clubs they advised, and seeking help as I applied to colleges.

Being a teacher was my dream. I wanted to inspire young minds, ignite a love for learning, and help kids discover their interests and passions just like some of my favorite teachers did for me. But the job wasn't what I thought it would be. Sure, I loved my students, and we did some incredible projects together. I was nominated for (and won!) several accolades,

1

including a Disney Creativity in Teaching award, and was awarded grants for projects that helped facilitate things like self-publishing a book of stories my students had written and throwing a launch party at a local bookstore, sponsoring a rookie musher in the Iditarod and learning to sew the special booties the dogs wore to protect their paws from the ice, and painting a life-sized game board on the ceiling tiles of my classroom so the kids could "play the room."

More and more, though, instead of spending most of my days nurturing curious minds and fostering creativity, I found myself required to administer an increasing number of tests, formative assessments, and screeners. My focus was forced to shift from building up kids, so they knew how to learn and achieve incredible things, to fixing problems, addressing deficits, and overcoming challenges. I had to find out what was *wrong* with each kiddo so I could figure out how to *fix* them. I hated it, but I didn't know there was an alternative at the time.

I left my teaching job to write full-time from home, thinking I'd work while my kids were in school, and then be there for them at the end of the school day to spend the afternoon and evenings nurturing their love of learning. Looking back, I can see how I was setting up the perfect situation for a future of homeschooling. I was taking on freelance assignments, writing books for teachers, parents, and kids, and had time during the day to make meals from scratch and bake cookies for an afterschool snack.

The Best Thing. . .

I like learning something every single day!
—Katherine, 10

As I researched for my assigned freelance projects, text book chapters, and classroom resources, I began to read work by John Taylor Gatto, Diane Ravitch, Charlotte Mason, Sir Ken Robinson, and more. My kids were these itty-bitty, curious beings whom I wanted more for, but didn't know what else to do besides send them to preschool, then move them on to our public elementary school, and enrich their brains and creativity once they were back home. It took watching my son Trevor's love of learning fade to wake me up to other options.

The Gift

When we walked out of that school for the last time after stopping by to grab a few things Trevor had realized were in the classroom, and with permission from his first-grade teacher to say goodbye to the class, we ran into his kindergarten teacher in the hall. She asked if Trevor was going home sick, and he told her that he was going to be homeschooled from now on.

I braced myself for her comments and was surprised when she bent down to give him a hug, then give me one in turn. She had tears in her eyes when she looked at us and said, "this will be a great thing for you Trevor. I can't wait to see all you do. Please keep in touch with me." She gave me another hug and whispered that I was doing the right thing for him, and then walked toward her classroom.

Over the years, we've had a mix of positive interactions like the one with Trevor's kindergarten teacher, and negative ones from others. I kept the kids in focus and did my best to let all opinions roll off my back in those early weeks as I knew in my gut we were doing the right thing, but still didn't know other homeschoolers. It wasn't always easy, and I'm *much* better about ignoring naysayers now.

Homeschooling has been the greatest gift I didn't know I needed. There have been so many advantages to bringing my son home, keeping the other three home, and learning alongside them for all these years. We're closer than I can imagine us being if they'd been gone all day, five days a week. They appreciate their siblings, and our family truly enjoys one another. But there are so many more advantages to homeschooling than just my own personal love of spending time with my family and engaging in a child-focused, strengths-based, creativity-rich, and critical-thinking fueled homeschool.

Cognitive Advantages

My sweet kiddo Logan struggled in a lot of areas when she was young. She was a sensory seeker, and always needed more. More movement, more noise, more stimulation, more, more, *more*. As we tried to figure out how to help her in the early years, she visited an occupational therapist, a child psychologist, a physical therapist, and others. The preschool and elementary years were filled with appointments, therapies, play groups, and supports to allow her to receive the help she needed in all the different areas in which she struggled.

She was eventually diagnosed with an alphabet soup, including sensory processing disorder, generalized anxiety disorder, dyslexia, and auditory processing disorder, while also displaying signs of creative giftedness and ADHD. She's a puzzle.

Because we homeschool and have the flexibility of designing our approach to learning to fit the kids we have, and by the time she came along, we'd been doing it a while, we decided to take a *better late than early* approach to Logan's education. All those appointments took time and effort and energy. Sometimes we'd be out of the house for hours and hours, five days a week. The other kids would do their schoolwork in the lobby of whatever office we were in while I entertained toddler Isaac and Logan met with her therapists.

The Best Thing. . .

I love getting time with my mom.

—Josiah, 8

The last thing she needed when we returned home was more work after her therapists worked on fine- and gross-motor skills, handwriting, worry, anticipation, input for the sensory seeking, and talked her through whatever big, scary things were currently keeping her up at night. And her dyslexia made it difficult for her to do work independently as reading and writing were tough, especially after using her brain so diligently at her appointments.

Instead, we gave her time to play once we returned home. We set her loose in the backyard with her brothers and sister, the neighbors who were home at the end of their school day, and the dogs. We put aside the math, handwriting, language arts, science, and history. All formal lessons were tabled, despite the current (Dad) and former (Mom) classroom teachers worrying she was "falling behind" her same-aged traditionally schooled peers, academically.

We didn't drill and practice math facts, have her write paragraphs, fill out lab manuals, or prove she could read through a list of sight words. Instead, we bought her art supplies and showed her how to look up drawing tutorials online because she loved to draw and imagine. We encouraged her to tell us stories and draw them while we wrote her dictated words on the pages of the little blank books she filled. We let go of the need to push, plug the holes in the content areas, and leaned heavily into the things she loved to do, was good at, and where she wanted to be.

Was this easy? No, but she thrived. When it was time for therapy or to work on the at-home exercises or tasks, she jumped in with enthusiasm because she'd spent so much time on the things she was good at, and her confidence soared.

Homeschooling isn't just an alternative to traditional education; it's a dynamic and flexible approach that you can tailor to suit your kiddos' unique needs and interests. One of the most obvious advantages of home-schooling is being able to personalize your children's academic experience to meet their individual needs. If your child is having difficulty in certain areas, is highly gifted, has ADHD or another learning challenge, or has any other neurodiversity, homeschooling can be adjusted to adapt to those needs. You and I can modify the curriculum so it fits our kiddo's preferred learning style, ensuring that our child receives the necessary support as well as the necessary challenges in order to flourish.

It puts us in the driver's seat when it comes to our child's education. We can handpick the curriculum and resources that best resonate with our child's interests and learning style. This means our child can progress at a pace that suits their individual readiness, rather than being confined to a rigid grade level. We can accelerate our advanced reader while letting them take their time with math – it's all about what works for them. Plus, we have the flexibility to craft a schedule that aligns with our child's needs and our family's lifestyle. In most states, you can even set your own graduation requirements, allowing your teenager to prepare for their unique path, whether it's work, a creative pursuit, entrepreneurship, the trades, or college.

With a low student-teacher ratio, we avoid time wasted on activities like standing in lines or waiting for others to finish. There's a wide variety of homeschooling styles and approaches to choose from, allowing us to engage in traditional styles of learning or focus on our child's passions. Many parents find that interest-led learning fosters well-rounded skills and knowledge across various subjects. Instead of dwelling on weaknesses, homeschooling emphasizes strengths-based learning. We can incorporate inquiry-based learning into our daily routine, nurturing our kiddos' critical thinking skills. And here's the best part: as parents, we're already the experts on our child's needs.

One of the greatest advantages is that we can place value on our kiddos' unique potential rather than sticking to standardized, minimum standards. This means breaking free from the constraints of standardized testing and aligning our homeschooling approach with what we know about child development. For example, young children learn best through play, and each child follows their own developmental timeline. Homeschooling can provide children with the freedom to continue building their knowledge even when their skills might be developing at a different pace. The beauty of homeschooling is that it eliminates many traditional school practices like excessive testing and grading, especially during the early years.

It goes beyond academics, though. Homeschooling prepares our children for life. Spending more time at home provides opportunities for our children to learn essential life skills such as cooking and budgeting. Learning to be an adult becomes an integral part of living and learning, setting them up for a more confident and capable future. For a teen dedicated to an all-consuming interest, such as training as an athlete or in the fine arts, homeschooling can provide a schedule that complements their intense training

and dedication. It offers the flexibility needed to pursue these passions to the fullest.

Our teens can prepare for college by cultivating transcripts that stand out for their unique experiences. They can follow their interests more deeply, making them attractive candidates for admissions. Plus, they often experience less burnout from busywork since they're able to focus on what truly matters in their educational journey. Teens who prefer to enter the workforce directly can concentrate on vocational training, checking out informal apprenticeships or mentorships during their high school years. Many young entrepreneurs find homeschooling advantageous, gaining business experience that they can apply to launching post-high school start-ups.

The Best Thing. . .

Getting to be home to do my own thing.
—Matthias, 19

Mental and Physical Health Advantages

It was the last day of a three-day convention, and I'd just finished talking about homeschooling kiddos with anxiety. I try to do a session on anxiety at every homeschool or parenting conference I attend as the rooms for those talks are always heartbreakingly full. Kids and their families are struggling and need support. As I was packing up my computer, a mom and her daughter approached the stage, hand in hand. I stopped what I was doing and went to the edge of the stage and sat so I was at their level.

The sweet girl looked at me and said, "I'm just like Logan. I worry all the time too. Will you tell her that I'm going to try some of the things you said she does? I think they might help me too." During my talks I share stories, all of them approved by the kids beforehand. My anxiety talks tend to have a lot of stories about Logan and how she manages her generalized anxiety disorder. She's attended these events with me before and has seen how her story helps kids and their parents, so she always likes me to talk about her.

I talked to that mom and daughter a few more times in passing that day and told them to keep in touch. About a week later, I received an email from the mom. She wrote about their drive home and how grateful she was that she and her daughter had sat in on my particular talk that day. When they were driving home, their car was hit by a driver who'd lost control of his truck. They weren't hurt too badly, but they were very shaken up.

While they waited for help to arrive, Mom sat with her sweet little girl and the two of them worked through some of the strategies they'd heard that afternoon, validating what each other was feeling, reassuring one another they were okay, applying deep pressure through long, extended hugs, and generally staying calm, breathing, and talking through it. It was one of the scariest things they'd ever gone through, made a little easier because they had the strategies they'd learned about alongside one another. They were a team in the truest sense, giving each other the best support they could in those moments, and lifting themselves up in the process.

Homeschooling allows us to normalize focusing on mental and emotional well-being, along with physical health. When our kids are grappling with anxiety, depression, sickness, injury, or any mental or physical health challenges, we can place therapy, coping skills, and medical care at the forefront. By addressing these issues proactively, we create a solid foundation for the holistic growth we hope to see in our children.

Sometimes, mental health struggles may be intertwined with a negative school environment. Trevor's first-grade experience was very damaging to his confidence and mental health. Homeschooling provided a lifeline to him. It meant liberation from trauma, a reduction in school-induced stress, a decrease in school refusal, and a deepening of self-acceptance and self-connection for him. Homeschooling empowers us to make an immediate choice to transform our children's learning environment for the better.

Research tells us that a key element of effective learning is a strong sense of autonomy, and homeschooling allows us to cultivate independence. We can give our kids freedom to participate in decisions about what and how they want to learn. They can explore their interests and curiosity without being bound by grades or the desire to please a teacher. But one of the most impactful mental health advantages of homeschooling for a struggling kiddo is simply being at home, surrounded by the people who love them most. Homeschooling prioritizes family bonds, providing a nurturing environment where our child's mental and emotional health are safeguarded.

Our kids can move more, play outside, indulge in activities like dance and sports, connect with nature, and even incorporate movement into their academic learning. Being this active fosters their physical health, strengthens mental health, and builds the confidence that comes with skill practice.

Around age thirteen, each of my kids started shifting their sleep schedules. They stay up a little later and sleep in much later. We can prioritize these sleep

needs. Our kids can enjoy more restorative sleep and wake up naturally with their sleep schedule adjusting to their activities. This flexibility is especially beneficial for teenagers as their body clocks shift, allowing them to stay up later and sleep in according to their natural rhythm. It's been a huge advantage for my musical theater kiddo. Being able to sleep in and alter her school schedule has given Molly the freedom to audition for musicals as far as an hour away, perform on professional stages, and take part in late-night rehearsals and performances. Her resume is impressive because she's able to shift her school and sleep schedules to accommodate her training and performing.

When Logan had pneumonia and was lethargic for weeks, we were able to shower her with compassion. She wasn't accumulating stacks of missing assignments, and she was still learning. She watched documentaries, listened to audiobooks, and focused on healing, recovery, and coping — well-being took precedence over academics. Homeschooling is a holistic journey that nurtures our children's physical health, mental health, and emotional well-being.

Social–Emotional Advantages

Before they decided to homeschool, Cora was worried about Serena. She worried she was wasting her daughter's childhood, constantly focused on remediation, driving her back and forth to therapies, doctors' visits, and tutoring. She felt the weight of all she couldn't do for fear of a meltdown, panic attack, or simple overwhelm. Cora decided to homeschool and vowed to change the narrative. She especially wanted Serena to remember her childhood and teenage years as a time when she could be herself and be accepted for who she was.

Cora wanted to boost Serena's social–emotional health and give her the time she needed to grow and mature at her own pace. She wanted Serena to have time to work on social skills. She knew she could incorporate social, emotional, and organizational skills into their everyday, giving Serena the support and love she needed to grow.

The Best Thing. . .

I like starting the day at my pace, getting my
work done, and then lots of time to work on my
own projects.

—Justus, 11

Homeschooling gives us an opportunity to foster healthy social development. Growing up in a homeschooling environment paves the way for extended family relationships. Parents, grandparents, and other relatives play a pivotal role as both role models and mentors. They instill values, help navigate conflicts positively, and guide our kids in their behavior. Trevor's best friend was my father-in-law. Grandpa Lenny loved model trains, and every Friday, his train club would come over to his house, work on the model railroad setup that filled the basement, eat whatever lunch one of the wives had sent over in a crockpot, then head home mid-afternoon. Because we homeschooled, Trevor was able to sleep over his grandpa's house two or three Thursdays a month so he could be there with all the old train guys and hang out with his friends.

He spent years working with Grandpa Lenny and the train guys, both in that basement and at train shows around northeast Ohio. When Grandpa Lenny became ill and we knew he wasn't going to recover, he directed us on how we could help the train guys dismantle and distribute the pieces of the setup. He'd earmarked something specific for each of his grandchildren and the rest was being divided up between his friends. Before they dismantled it, though, Trevor, a talented videographer, went over to record it for all those who'd worked on it. I'll never forget watching him and his elderly friends mourn together while they watched the video in the parlor of the funeral home on the day we buried Grandpa Lenny.

Homeschooling allows for our kids to find mentors within the family and outside of it. They become friends with people based on their interests and can cultivate cross-generational partnerships that help them develop into compassionate and nurturing young adults.

Learning extends into the real world. It emphasizes community engagement and involvement. Our kids have the time to volunteer, vote alongside us, and participate in various community activities with peers and individuals of all ages and backgrounds. Homeschooling nurtures not only the intellect, but also the heart and hands, promoting a holistic approach to social-emotional development. My girls have started volunteering as teacher's aides in several preschool acting classes at the fine arts center where they perform, and one of them has found a natural gift for working with special needs preschoolers. She intuitively buddied up with the little boy in the class with the highest needs and focuses her attention on him, while her sister and the teacher lead the others through the activities.

Perhaps the greatest advantage of homeschooling, though, is that it is all about our kids. I remember when I first started teaching. We were told to weigh every plan we made against the research to choose what was best for kids. By the time I left teaching, that wasn't the case, universally. We could do what was best for kids, if it was the same thing the other teachers in the grade level were doing so it stayed fair. All classrooms in a grade level needed to do the same projects, read the same books, and write the same papers because we now had to make sure all kids were equal. But once the creativity goes out of teaching, we know we don't grow lifelong learners. Keeping everything the same means we can't use our natural gifts to inspire students. It meant I couldn't implement projects like the Iditarod program, the self-publishing adventure, or any of the other unique challenges my students and I enjoyed. If all third graders weren't doing it, we couldn't either. Which means that the sweet little third grader I had who began to see herself as a writer after the bookstore signing we did as a class would have never become a published children's author. How many other kiddos are missing that spark of inspiration a creative teacher could fuel by bringing innovation into the classroom?

We can light those sparks in our own kids, though. Better, we can see the little embers of interest when our kiddos find something they enjoy and offer more opportunities to grow in that area. Who knows what flame that opportunity will spark? When we homeschool, we can look at each kiddo in front of us, get to know who they are, what makes them tick, how they think, learn, and feel, and then design the educational experience that is perfect for them. It's like we can write an educational prescription for each of the kids in our home, meet them where they are, build on their strengths, cultivate their curiosity, and ignite a love of learning in them that will last a lifetime.

Try This!

- **Personalize learning:** If your child struggles with traditional math, use everyday examples like cooking to teach math concepts.
- **Be flexible:** Adapt the schedule to align with your child's natural rhythms. Let your teens sleep in later to accommodate their changing sleep patterns.
- **Focus on strengths:** Instead of fixating on your child's weaknesses, emphasize their strengths and interests. If your child loves music, encourage music pursuits to boost their confidence and expertise.
- **Nurture critical thinking:** Encourage your child to ask questions and deeply explore topics.
- **Focus on needs:** Enjoy the freedom from excessive standardized testing. Focus on your child's developmental timeline and unique learning needs.
- **Teach life skills:** Teach your kids essential adult skills practically, like cooking and budgeting.
- **Customize transcripts:** Help your teens create distinctive transcripts that impress college admissions. Highlight their interests, passions, and in-depth learning experiences.
- **Prioritize mental health:** Make your child's mental health a priority by addressing anxiety, depression, or other challenges proactively. This may involve therapy, coping strategies, and mental health support.
- **Focus on rest and recovery:** When your child is sick or recovering, prioritize rest and healing without the pressure of schoolwork. Let them watch documentaries, listen to audiobooks, and focus on recovery.

- **Foster social development:** Have your child learn from grand-parents, neighbors, friends, and relatives. They can build strong connections with family members of all ages.
- **Engage with the community:** Encourage your child to participate in community activities, volunteer, and engage with peers of all ages.
- **Support children with anxiety:** Work alongside your child to develop coping skills.

2 | Exploring Strengths

The key to human development is building on who you already are.
—Tom Rath

The moment you doubt whether you can fly, you cease forever to be able to do it.
—From *Peter Pan* by J.M. Barrie

When Noah was in high school, he was enrolled in an environmental science class because he didn't want to take chemistry and had already enjoyed biology. Environmental science, with its focus on real-world issues he cared deeply about, seemed more engaging to him than chemistry, so his parents scouted for an environmental science class locally that he could participate in as a homeschooled high schooler.

He struggled, though, when it came time to work on the end-of-semester project. He was challenged to design a presentation depicting a way to make life sustainable on Mars based on his understanding of environmental science. He struggled with the presentation format and faced overwhelming feelings of frustration and a lack of confidence when attempting to break down the extensive project into manageable parts. He had a "must complete everything now" mindset. In response, his parents came alongside him, demonstrating how to chunk a big project into smaller, achievable tasks.

But even after learning to break down the project into manageable parts with support, he disliked the prescribed way of submitting the assignment. His parents, once again, came alongside of him, this time to brainstorm alternative ideas for sharing his knowledge. Ultimately, he chose to ask his teacher if using Minecraft to demonstrate his understanding was an acceptable option. The beauty of advocating in this way is that it helps kids understand that what matters most is demonstrating awareness and mastery of a subject, and not the specific method of presentation. Noah's parents encouraged him to showcase his knowledge in a way that aligns with his unique abilities and interests.

In public and private schools, children often struggle to advocate for such personalized learning, but when we homeschool, we have the freedom to explore diverse educational paths. If you have a child like Noah who loves video games, maybe having him show what he's learned by building it in Minecraft is something that will motivate him. Or, if you have a kiddo who is very visually-spatially adept, they could build a model of what they've learned with LEGO. The possibilities are endless when we focus on individualizing the methods we use to facilitate learning in our homeschool. Too often, though, we default to conventional methods of teaching and learning because they are familiar. It's crucial to recognize that we can provide our children with the freedom to express their learning differently.

The Best Thing. . .

Getting to do projects that I come up with
that reflect what I'm learning and directing my
own learning.

—Isaac, 13

Noah bravely went ahead and suggested the idea of a Minecraft presentation to his teacher. Remarkably, she not only accepted it, but also identified other students who were struggling with the assignment and proposed he collaborate with them. This recommendation took a child who had initially resisted the assignment and turned him into someone eager to work with others. It leveraged his love for connecting and collaborating with peers and gave him the opportunity to thrive in a team setting as a leader. It gave him the chance for creative expression, something he couldn't find in the initial structure of the project's scope.

Not only did he and his team meet the minimum project requirements specified in the rubric, but they went far beyond in terms of time investment and attention to detail. They had so much fun working together that they pushed the boundaries of their presentation. The teacher was so impressed with their creativity and teamwork that she used their work as an example for other students. This experience boosted his confidence and leadership skills, as he led a team to accomplish a shared goal. Above all, it was validating for his parents to witness his increased confidence and his growth as a student and a young leader.

A Strengths-Based Learning Approach

A strengths-based approach to learning is an educational approach that focuses on identifying and nurturing a child's individual strengths, talents, and interests as the primary means of promoting their academic and personal development. When we apply this approach to our parenting and homeschooling, we work to shift our perspective from a deficit-based model, which identifies and addresses weaknesses and challenges, to a model that emphasizes our child's existing abilities and passions.

Like Noah's parents demonstrated, with a strengths-based approach, we look for and celebrate our kiddos' unique strengths, whether they are academic, artistic, athletic, social, or emotional. These strengths could include talents in subjects like math, science, writing, art, music, or even skills like leadership, empathy, or creativity.

Strengths-based learning reminds us that every child is different and learns in their own way. When I look at my four kids, I can't imagine how I used to teach a classroom of twenty or more children, all with different needs. My four are enough of a challenge. My oldest, now a graduate of our homeschool, learns best when he can dive deeply into his topic of choice and watch videos, tutorials, and test things out on his own. Ask him to read or write about it, and he rebelled. My second kiddo is a performer through and through. She's also linguistic, articulate, and taught herself to read by age three. She can absorb anything through the written or spoken word, but ask her to manage numbers and she falls apart. My younger two think and learn about their world differently still. As homeschooling parents, we can create personalized learning plans that leverage our kiddos' strengths.

We can tailor assignments, projects, or extracurricular activities to align with the child's interests and talents. For example, my performer has taken acting classes, worked with private dance and voice coaches, volunteered in summer camps and preschool theater classes, and studied scripts as literature. She's written short one-act plays and entered contests and explored a variety of subject areas through the lens of the performing arts.

When we encourage our children to explore and develop their strengths, their confidence and self-esteem soar. They develop a positive self-image that can have a profound impact on their motivation to learn and achieve. They take risks, try new things, and see failure as an opportunity to learn. They're also motivated. When kids spend their time immersed in areas of strength and focused on interests, they develop intrinsic motivation. They enjoy learning for its own sake, and when children are passionate about what they're learning, they are more likely to be engaged and invested in their education.

The Best Thing. . .

You can choose what to learn and do it in
your own way.

—Diego, 15

While strengths-based learning primarily emphasizes strengths, it doesn't mean homeschooling parents ignore weaknesses or challenges. Instead, we focus on weaknesses in a constructive way, helping our kids build necessary skills and overcome obstacles. When we nurture our kids through their strengths, we build trust and strengthen our communication with them. We can have meaningful conversations about their learning, hobbies they might enjoy pursuing, and the goals that they have for their future.

Strengths-based learning promotes a lifelong love of learning. When children are encouraged to pursue their passions and interests, they are more likely to continue learning throughout their lives. In essence, creating a strengths-based homeschool involves recognizing, nurturing, and supporting our children's unique talents and interests, fostering more engaged and confident learners who are better equipped to face any challenges they have in life.

You may be thinking, this whole strengths-based idea is great, but what happens when our kids get out in the real world and need to do hard things? If they spend all their time doing the things they love, focusing on their interests, and only leaning into their strengths, what happens when a parent isn't there to smooth the way for them and things get hard?

Well, when we spend our time parenting and homeschooling in a way that builds up our kids, creating a safe place to makes mistakes, our kids rise to the challenges they face, even those outside of our homes. We seem to be ignoring what research – and our own experiences – keep telling us in favor of what we were brought up to believe about how learning should work. In the traditional model of education, we treat all subjects equally.

A report card has letter grades for each subject, and they all count the same to calculate your overall grade point average. Math is just as important as history, science, and even PE or drama. This means that kids need to focus most of their effort on the subjects in which they struggle, the ones that aren't their strengths, so they can avoid pulling down their overall average. They end up spending a lot of time trying to improve in areas where they're not naturally strong.

Despite what our educational system would have you believe; this isn't a reflection of real life. Adults don't pick careers that require them to be *just okay*. They choose jobs that match their interests and strengths. I'm not a biologist, despite having to spend just as much time on science during my school years as someone who is. In fact, I read an article the other day on *Medium* entitled, "Yes, You Should Major in Theatre." The author, Matt Fotis, boldly claims, "No other major, including business, better prepares you to enter the 21st century workforce" because it "makes you a better human being." He goes on to explain that theater majors learn empathy, resilience, visual aesthetics, storytelling, acceptance, and adaptability among other, more technical and academic skills.

The article presents a perfect metaphor of theater for strengths-based homeschooling because when we allow our kids to spend more time on their strong subjects, they tend to do much better in all areas, even the ones they're not so great at. This is because when they learn deeply in their strong areas, they start applying that knowledge to their weaker subjects.

Rooted in Positive Psychology

Strengths-based learning is rooted in a field of study that focuses on nurturing the positive aspects of the parent-child relationship and promoting overall well-being. This field is known as positive psychology, and it offers a fresh and illuminating perspective on how we can raise happy, resilient, and emotionally healthy children. Unlike traditional psychology, which often concentrates on identifying and addressing problems and disorders, positive psychology delves into the science of what makes life fulfilling and meaningful. It explores the strengths, virtues, and positive emotions that can be harnessed to improve the quality of our lives and those of our children.

In the late 1990s, Dr. Martin Seligman noticed that most of the popular approaches to psychology focused on the negative. While he acknowledged that this was necessary to providing treatment, he also reported that other areas, like promoting optimal functioning, were neglected. He felt that psychologists were most interested in pathologizing patients, or finding out what was wrong, instead of focusing on what they were already doing well and could use to improve other areas. He felt that what is adaptive about people was understudied. Seligman challenged the American Psychological Association's members to become invested in identifying patients' strengths to enhance their lives, and the idea of positive psychology was born.

Seligman defines *positive psychology* as "the scientific study of the strengths that enable individuals and communities to thrive. The field is founded on the belief that people want to lead meaningful and fulfilling lives, to cultivate what is best within themselves, and to enhance their experiences of love, work, and play." Seligman's objective was to promote a different perspective that emphasizes the affirmative aspects of human nature. Positive psychology, as a result, explores subjects like joy, adaptability, hopefulness, self-worth, and the highest levels of human performance.

The Best Thing. . .

The best is being able to eat whenever you want!

—Keira, 13

Using concepts from positive psychology, coupled with a strengths-based approach, we can foster a nurturing, thriving, and joyful homeschool environment. This approach to homeschooling promotes resilience, builds strong family connections, and helps our children not just survive, but thrive in an increasingly complex world.

Parenting can feel like a rollercoaster ride filled with exhilarating highs and daunting lows, and homeschooling is that rollercoaster ride *on steroids*. It's a path filled with incredible joys, but it also comes with its fair share of challenges. The idea that we are responsible for every part of our kiddos' upbringing, education, and development is overwhelming at times.

Fortunately, when we truly lean into the idea of being there as our kids discover their world, we do what Seligman encouraged and focus on the good, navigating the adventure with optimism, resilience, and joy. Let's explore how the principles of positive psychology can positively impact your homeschool journey.

Cultivating Resilience and Gratitude

One of the core tenets of positive psychology is resilience, the ability to bounce back from adversity. Twelve-year-old Mateo's mom worried about his ability to deal with disappointment when a lunar eclipse was to be visible overhead during the rainy season in Mexico City where they lived. Mateo is obsessed with space and had been hoping to see an eclipse for most of his young life. From June through October, though, it's common for them to have rain and clouds all day and night around the clock. There was going to be a lunar eclipse during this season and its peak of visibility over Mexico City was expected to be around 3:00 a.m. local time. Mateo was pumped, and so family members set their alarms, put their coats and binoculars by the door, and had everything ready to go to up to the roof to try and catch the eclipse. Mateo, a very bright, but sensitive kiddo, often built things up in his head to the point he'd feel tremendous let-down, followed by outbursts and depression if things didn't go according to the picture he'd painted in his head. His mom knew it would be very important to manage his expectations because they might not be able to see anything if it were cloudy, a scenario that was highly likely at this time of the morning in the heart of the rainy season.

When the alarm woke him up on the morning of the eclipse, he danced excitedly into his parents' room, pouncing on the bed to wake them up. They trekked up to the roof, settled in, hunkering together in the misty rain, and looked at the cloudy sky, hoping to see a break. Mateo was thrilled to see a tiny hole in the clouds where they could just make out the dusty red moon right in its center. He had less than a minute to enjoy the sight he'd waited his short life to see, as the clouds connected, blanketing the entire sky for the rest of the day. His mom braced herself for the sweep of disappointment she knew was coming; after all, he'd had a tiny taste of what he'd waited to see and may not have the opportunity to see a total lunar eclipse again. As she turned toward Mateo, she was shocked to find her arms full of her delighted son who declared this "the best night of my life."

As parents, we want our children to be strong, to face life's challenges with courage, and to learn from setbacks. Resilience can be nurtured. Mateo's mom and dad had spent the time leading up to the eclipse working their way through scenarios they might face while out on that roof in the early morning, with most of their roleplays being centered on not actually seeing even a slight glimpse of the eclipse he so desperately wanted to see. By spending the time homeschooling allows us to, figuring out what makes our kids tick, how they think, what their triggers are, and how to talk them through disappointments before, during, and after they happen, we empower them to face life's hurdles with determination.

Homeschooling through a strengths-based approach infused with the tenets of Seligman's psychology allows us time to cultivate positive emotions in our kids. In the hustle and bustle of daily life, it's easy to get caught up in stress, frustration, and negativity. However, by intentionally focusing on positive emotions like gratitude, kindness, and joy, we can create a more harmonious and joyful family environment. Take time to express gratitude as a family, either at the dinner table or before bedtime. Share what you're thankful for, no matter how big or small. This practice not only fosters appreciation, but also strengthens family bonds.

The Best Thing. . .

The best part of homeschooling is being able to read books I'm interested in and the flexibility to dive into projects that I love doing and learning about – and calling that school!

—Tyler, 17

My oldest son, Trevor, can be a bit of a doom-and-gloom personality. He comes by it honestly as my husband, bless his heart, excels in looking for the gray clouds within the silver linings. He's good at balancing my impulsive *let's-do-it-now-and-figure-it-out-as-we-go-along* personality and gives the kids the opportunity to see both sides of every issue. But Trevor takes the pessimism to a new level. Because of this, we started having table conversations when the kids were young, and still do now. I'll ask everyone at the table to talk about something great that happened during the day, then go around the table so everyone can share. We'll then share something horrible that happened, something we were each grateful for, and something we learned. The majority of what we share is positive, so when the kids share something horrible, or silly, or disappointing, it is tempered with the good, showing them that more positive things happen each day than negative when they look for them.

When we train ourselves and our kids to focus on the good, we find more good. When we focus on the negative, as Seligman found, we pathologize our lives and are always trying to fix problems.

Positive psychology encourages a strengths-based approach to parenting. Instead of constantly trying to fix what's wrong, look for and nurture your child's unique strengths and talents. Help them to develop their passions and interests. Every child is unique. Just like the beautiful melody that results when different instruments in an orchestra play their part, each child's strengths can complement those of their siblings, creating a harmonious family dynamic. Encourage them to explore their interests, whether it's art, sports, academics, theater, music, or whatever.

This perspective shift also emphasizes the importance of strong, positive relationships. Nurture your connection with your children through quality time together, active listening, and open communication. The beauty of homeschooling is that you have more time with your kids, and more time to build those connections. Take advantage of that. Relationships are built on trust and understanding. Remember, it's not just about the quantity of time you spend with your children, but the quality of that time. Put away your devices, engage in conversations, and create memorable experiences together. These moments of togetherness are the building blocks of strong relationships.

By embracing the principles of positive psychology, you can transform your parenting experience. You'll not only raise resilient, confident children but also create a happy, thriving home filled with love and positivity. As parents, we have the incredible opportunity to shape the future by nurturing the well-being of our children. By embracing the science of happiness, we can craft a beautiful journey of parenting that leaves a lasting positive impact on our children's lives, no matter how their brains are wired.

Helping Neurodivergent Kiddos

Jenn's daughter had been enrolled in a total of five schools in two countries. She had tried different schools with different methodologies: parochial, traditional, social constructivist, and so on, but things were not working. Elizabeth was regularly having meltdowns at school, and Jenn was routinely called to pick her up early. They spent many hours in the car, coming and going from therapies and appointments because, according to the experts, *school was not the problem, Elizabeth was.*

One morning, as Jenn was preparing Elizabeth's school lunch, she asked herself what she was doing. She thought about her goals for Elizabeth, and what she wanted to achieve by sending her to school. She realized that what she really wanted for her daughter was that she know who she is, was confident in herself, appreciated what her strengths and weaknesses were, and learned how to use those strengths to help her get through difficult times. School was not moving Elizabeth toward the goals her mother had for her. In fact, her teachers' focus on what was wrong with Elizabeth was taking its toll. Elizabeth was withdrawn, argumentative, and could barely be motivated to get out of bed in the morning without a fight.

Jenn and her family moved to the United States, where she met a neighbor, Kate, who homeschooled her very quirky kids. Kate's children were bright, social, and well adjusted. They welcomed the family into the neighborhood and invited Elizabeth to play with them from the moment they met. Jenn was intrigued and spent hours with Kate, talking about learning, socialization, and curriculum options. Kate told Jenn that her family chose to homeschool when their first child taught himself to read as a toddler. Her children were very smart, and Kate knew that the local school wouldn't be able to accommodate for their needs. Jenn's experience with Kate prompted her to give homeschooling a try. She knew Elizabeth was smart and that she also struggled with some sensory challenges and anxiety, but thought homeschooling might be the answer to meeting her needs.

The Best Thing. . .

I have friends of all ages – some much younger than me, and some much older. I like having the opportunity and courage to connect with people over what we have in common rather than simply our ages.

—Amelie, 14

When she started to plan their first homeschool year, she asked Elizabeth what she wanted to learn, expecting the ten-year-old fifth grader to tell her she wanted to learn science and history, and to stop doing math. She was surprised when Elizabeth asked if they could learn German, coding, and how to run her own business. As she shifted her thinking to what made up a traditional school lesson, and dove into the topics Elizabeth was interested in, she watched her neurodivergent daughter bloom.

Neurodivergent kiddos are those whose brains are wired in ways that are different from what is considered typical, or *neurotypical*. It includes a wide range of diagnoses, including autism, ADHD, dyslexia, sensory processing disorder, anxiety, giftedness, and more. Each neurodivergent child's experience is unique, and not all face the same challenges or strengths.

It's important to remember that neurodivergence is not a disorder, nor is it something that needs to be *fixed*. Instead, it's a natural variation of the human brain, akin to the diversity in our physical appearance and personality. In this sense, neurodiversity should be celebrated, appreciated, and respected for the richness it brings to our communities and families. However, since schools are structured to teach to the majority, neurodivergent kiddos tend to struggle in a classroom, and more and more parents are pulling their neurodivergent children to give them the education they deserve — at home.

Neurodivergent kiddos contribute so much to our world, and homeschooling allows parents to nurture those special traits like creativity, attention to detail, and unique perspectives. By doing so, we foster a more inclusive environment that values the unique qualities each person brings to the table, contributing to a more diverse and vibrant world. While neurodiversity should be celebrated and our kids need to know that they're exactly who they're meant to be, some neurodivergent children may require support or accommodations to help them thrive in various aspects of academics and life. This might involve individualized teaching strategies, therapy, or modifications to curriculum. Understanding these needs and working to meet them can make a significant difference in a neurodivergent kiddo's life.

Once Jenn embraced a strengths-based, positive homeschool style for Elizabeth, she no longer melted down over getting up in the morning. Jenn discovered that Elizabeth thrived when she had a say in planning her education and was willing to go along with subjects that are not her favorites because she knows it will balance with things that she loves. She was better able to regulate her emotions after only a few months, and she talked more animatedly at the dinner table in the evenings. She asked to join a local theater class and played outside with the neighbors every afternoon if they were home.

This is no surprise as NHERI (the National Home Education Research Institute) tells us in a summary of research published in 2023 that homeschooled children tend to shine when it comes to their social, emotional, and psychological development. They often surpass average in many ways. This includes things like making friends, feeling good about themselves, showing leadership qualities, enjoying strong family relationships, getting involved in community service, and having healthy self-esteem.

Homeschooling is a real game-changer for all kids as we'll talk about throughout this book, but it's especially beneficial for neurodivergent children. It's all about embracing the personal and unique journey of each child. One of the most beautiful aspects, as Elizabeth's story shows, is that neurodivergent children can set their own pace when it comes to their studies. This flexibility and the unique approach to learning means they can dive into their passions and interests, things that often get pushed aside in traditional schools. This exploration helps them uncover their true selves and gain self-awareness at an earlier age.

In the homeschooling world, they get the chance to interact with kids and adults in a way that's not always possible in regular schools. It's like they fast-track those essential life skills. And let's not forget the precious family time – parents get to be there every step of the way, strengthening those bonds with their kids. It's a beautiful journey of growth and discovery, particularly when we tap into our children's strengths.

Finding Our Children's Strengths

When Logan was in elementary school, she desperately wanted to write stories. She would spin tales for the neighbors, her little brother, and anyone else who would listen, but she grew increasingly frustrated as she tried to write her stories down in the little blank books I bought her in bulk. Her struggles with dyslexia made it a challenge for her to write and spell.

She loved listening to audiobooks and having stories read to her, but she froze up when having to write on her own.

Since she was good at drawing, and didn't mind the actual work of writing, I bought her an Amazon Echo Dot to put in our dining room where we did our school and artwork. When she wanted to work on a story, she would sit near the Echo and ask Alexa to spell words for her. Homeschooling offers a wonderful opportunity for parents to truly understand and cultivate their child's strengths. Logan excels in storytelling, so by giving her strategies to indulge in that area of strength while accommodating her weaknesses, she's able to continue to grow and learn in ways that make her feel successful.

The Best Thing. . .

I have so much time each day to do my own
thing and even my school work is planned around
topics I love and want to get better at.

—Cohen, 12

Traditional schools can make children feel like they must fit into predefined molds, but as a homeschooling parent, you can uncover your child's talents and interests within a nurturing and loving environment. But how can a parent figure out what their child's strengths are? It can be a challenge, but when you embrace your role of becoming a student of your child, you can identify and nurture your child's strengths through meaningful conversations, patience, and a warm atmosphere.

The first step in recognizing your child's strengths is to engage in open and honest conversations. Create an environment where your child feels comfortable expressing themselves without fear of judgment. Pose open-ended questions and genuinely listen to their responses. This can help you gain insights into their interests and passions. For example, ask your kiddo what they're most curious about or what subject gets them excited. We keep a large chart-sized Post-it® on the wall in our dining room with the question, *what do you want to learn about* written on it with a container of markers set nearby. My kids add to the chart throughout the school year, and we tackle a new topic as often as we can. Conversations sparked from questions like these can be a valuable window into your child's interests and strengths.

After I returned home from a conference I'd spoken at, I received an email from Karin, mama to profoundly gifted, intensely curious, and incredibly perfectionistic seven-year-old Brenna. Karin wrote:

I've been thinking of your idea of becoming a student of your child and I remember when Brenna asked about how her stepsister, my husband's daughter from his first marriage, could have the same father but not the same mother. That sparked conversations about genetics, prompting me to add "The Cartoon Guide to Genetics" book into our science reading loop, then put together a Knex model of DNA. We were able to explore a sophisticated topic without things that were construct irrelevant. We didn't use a curriculum for genetics because curricula for a topic like that would have been designed for high schoolers who could understand concepts at a much more sophisticated level. So, we read a cartoon guide in small sections, built a model, and let Brenna's questions take us down rabbit trails for answers. I guess my point is that if a child has an interest in a topic that is typically considered too sophisticated for the child's age, a solution is not to look for curriculum, but to let the experience be more of an exploration. There doesn't have to be a goal at the end, a final exam. It's okay for the experience to just give the child something big and meaty to wonder about and give them exposure to new vocabulary and concepts to which they'll make later connections.

Karin's willingness to meet her daughter where she was, help her learn something that was interesting to her but on her level, and tune in to the areas of strength (i.e., learning through books and hands-on models) allowed her to validate Brenna's question and quest for knowledge, helping her to learn something new in a relevant way, while not getting bogged down by a need to prove knowledge through a test or project at the end. She watched and listened, responding to her observations of her child.

Observation is a powerful tool in the process of discovering your child's strengths. Pay close attention to what your child naturally gravitates toward and finds joy in doing. Are they spending hours engrossed in their art, enthusiastically building things, or diving deep into a specific subject? Encourage them to explore these interests further. For example, if your

child loves creating art, provide them with the necessary materials and a dedicated space to nurture their artistic talents. Something as simple as setting up an art corner in your home with supplies like paints, paper, and sketchbooks can make a significant difference. The more they explore their interests, the easier it becomes to identify their strengths.

Try This!

- **Engage in open conversations:** Encourage your child to express their interests, curiosities, and passions. Ask open-ended questions like, "What do you enjoy doing the most?" or "What subjects make you excited to learn?"
- **Observe their natural inclinations:** Pay attention to how your child spends their free time. Do they frequently draw, tinker with gadgets, or immerse themselves in books? These activities can reveal their interests and strengths.
- **Provide diverse learning experiences:** Offer a range of subjects and activities to expose your child to various fields of knowledge.
- **Encourage hands-on exploration:** Let your child engage in hands-on learning experiences like conducting science experiments, creating art, or building projects.

- **Maintain a curiosity chart:** Create a visual representation, like a curiosity chart on the wall, where your child can add topics or subjects they want to learn more about.
- **Adapt your approach:** Be flexible in your homeschooling approach. If your child's interests change, be ready to adjust the curriculum to align with their current passions.
- **Encourage self-directed learning:** Allow your child to explore topics of interest and guide their own research and projects.
- **Seek opportunities for skill development:** If you notice a specific area in which your child excels, seek out opportunities for them to develop and refine those skills. This might involve enrolling them in specialized classes, finding mentors, or participating in related extracurricular activities.
- **Encourage exploration of diverse subjects:** Introduce your child to a wide range of subjects and fields, even those that may not seem directly related to their current interests. You never know when they might discover a new passion in an unexpected area.
- **Be patient and persistent:** Some strengths may not reveal themselves immediately. Keep encouraging your child to explore different interests over time and be patient as they discover what truly resonates with them.
- **Foster a growth mindset:** Emphasize that effort and perseverance are essential for growth, and setbacks are opportunities to learn and improve.
- **Connect with other homeschoolers:** Join homeschooling communities or groups where your child can interact with peers who have similar interests.
- **Use online resources:** Leverage online platforms, courses, and educational websites to expand your child's access to various subjects and resources.
- **Emphasize the joy of learning:** Make sure the learning process is enjoyable and filled with curiosity. When children find joy in what they're doing, they are more likely to excel and develop their strengths.

3 | Finding Wonder

Let us come alive to the splendor that is all around us, and see the beauty in ordinary things.

—Thomas Merton

It is only with the heart that one can see rightly; what is essential is invisible to the eye.

—From *The Little Prince* by Antoine de Saint-Exupéry

I often say that I came into the world of homeschooling kicking and screaming. It was not something I planned, and the choice to homeschool was thrust on me because of circumstance, some of which I've already discussed in the Introduction, and availability. You see, I'd left teaching with the idyllic plan to write full-time while raising my children. I'd have a mother's helper come to tend the younger ones while my oldest were in school, and I'd have plenty of time to meet my deadlines, bake cookies for an afterschool snack, and be the involved mother I'd always planned to be.

When it became clear that the only choice we had for our outside-the-box, extreme thinking first grader was to pull him out of the local public school and teach him at home, I was overwhelmed and underprepared. Don't misunderstand: now, after more than a decade and a half of homeschooling my children, graduating that quirky kiddo who made me both a mom and a homeschooler, with three more kiddos at home, I don't think any amount of preparation replaces a heart for your kids and trusting yourself to know what they need, when they need it.

The first year Trevor was at home was both incredible and terrible. I'd been freelancing from home for a little over a year, which is what allowed our family to make the choice to homeschool him in the first, and had a local neighborhood mom coming to the house three mornings a week to help out with two-year-old Molly and nursing-infant Logan. The sitter wasn't a fan of homeschooling as she felt that kids just belonged in a traditional school setting because that was simply what was done, and she made her opinion clear. I suspect part of her attitude toward our decision to homeschool was rooted in the mistaken assumption that by choosing to homeschool our child, we were passing judgment on those whose kids attended the school we pulled Trevor from, the same school her daughter currently attended. Oftentimes parents who don't understand homeschooling, know much about it, or think they'd never homeschool their own kids feel as if homeschoolers are judging their choices. Interestingly, I think most people – homeschooling or not – are actually thinking more about what others think of them than what others are *actually* thinking of them. My babysitter was wrong. I wasn't thinking about her educational decisions, or anyone else's, when I pulled Trevor out of school. I was thinking of my own child and what was best for him. She was a nice woman, but insecure about her parenting and career choices, and unfortunately, she took that out on our family once Trevor came home to learn, so I tried to keep him with me during the mornings she was at the house watching the girls. I put up a little school desk in my office and pulled out the workbooks Trevor had brought home with him. I figured we could work together for those few hours each week.

The Best Thing. . .

I get to have friends over all the time and can
do my school work outside or even on the
trampoline.

—Erik, 9

What a mistake. I was doing what so many homeschool parents do when they choose to bring their kids home from a school setting – trying to replicate school at home. I was putting my movement-driven learner in a desk for hours at a time and giving him workbook pages. I forgot that the reason we'd brought Trevor home in the first place was that the traditional model of learning wasn't working for him.

When it comes to our kids' education, there's something truly magical about nontraditional approaches. They're like a key that unlocks the door to a personalized learning adventure, tailored to your child's unique strengths, interests, and needs. Not every kiddo thrives in a traditional school setting. Some find it challenging to fit into the strict rules and the structured routine, and that can lead to a lack of enthusiasm and struggles with academics. This is exactly why homeschooling was such a disaster for us over the first couple of months; I wasn't changing up things in the way Trevor needed me to.

Changing up things starts to feel like a breath of fresh air for our wonderfully creative or delightfully unconventional children who don't quite fit the traditional mold, and so I leaned into this idea of doing things differently. I put the books away, sent Trevor out to play with his sister, the neighbors, and the babysitter for those few hours a week I had her, and we spent all our other time over the remainder of that school year exploring parks, zoos, libraries, and museums in northeast Ohio.

Following Interests and Rabbit Trails

When Trevor and I finally sat down to talk about what he wanted to learn that first year, he was thrilled to tell me he'd always wanted to learn more about space. I decided to lean all the way into the idea of capitalizing on his strengths and interests, and following his lead, so we started digging for resources together. His passion and drive were two of his strengths, that ability to perseverate on a topic born out of his ADHD and intellectual overexcitabilities, so I let him loose in the library. While he peppered the children's librarian with questions and she guided him toward books of all levels, I sat in the playroom letting the baby nap and the toddler play while I looked up unit study ideas on my laptop, bookmarking the most appealing.

I didn't want to spend a lot of money up front as I wasn't sure how long he'd be interested in outer space, or how deep he'd want to go. I knew I wanted to integrate as many subject areas as possible into that one topic so it would not only seem like fun to him, but it could also serve to reignite the spark that had been extinguished in the first-grade classroom he'd left the year before. Math was a strength, so we decided together that he'd just continue with the workbooks I'd found for him so he could progress at his own pace, and I wouldn't have to worry about getting creative with it. He loved to learn through hands-on activities, videos, and by talking to people, so we earmarked videos to watch, experiments to do, and found a local amateur astronomical society and started attending its meetings.

Encouraging your children's curiosity and tailoring your homeschooling approach to align with their interests can be a powerful way to motivate both your kids and you. This approach makes homeschooling more engaging, interesting, and passion-driven. While it may initially seem overwhelming, it's not as challenging as it appears on the surface if you're open to thinking creatively. It's worth emphasizing that following your children's interests is especially effective for fostering a love of learning, particularly in neurodivergent children, whether they are gifted, have anxiety, sensory sensitivities, are on the autism spectrum, or face learning challenges like dyslexia, dysgraphia, or dyscalculia. When children are genuinely interested in a subject, they become more motivated to learn, which can also help them overcome obstacles more readily.

The Best Thing. . .

I can play and draw with my brothers every day.

—Nora, 4

Since that first astronomy deep dive, I've loved following rabbit trails with my kids over the years. Sometimes, as is the case with the astronomy unit, we've culminated the learning with a project like a lapbook, video, research paper, booklet, or presentation. Other times we've learned about a topic of interest or tried new experiments for the sole pleasure of exploring a new thing and just talking about it.

The goal is to nurture your kids' innate curiosity and keep it alive throughout their lives. By starting this when they're young, you can instill a natural inclination to seek knowledge as they grow into adulthood. The aim is to empower them to be proactive learners who know that the information they desire is just a click away, and they won't hesitate to ask questions or confront their shortcomings. This approach prepares them to be lifelong learners, unafraid to seek knowledge independently.

For instance, when my kids were younger, we explored history through a flexible curriculum we used as a spine or jumping off point. If a topic piqued their interest, we delved into related activities. We spent more than the prescribed year on the first book because my kids were captivated by ancient Egypt. They absorbed everything about mummies, pharaohs, pyramids, and Egypt's culture. This passion extended to their art, play, and other subjects, effectively covering various subject areas.

When your child's interest is sparked, you can enhance their learning experience by conducting simple online searches, reading blogs, watching videos, and exploring books and resources related to the topic. This holistic approach ensures that your children naturally engage with multiple subjects. You don't need to add extra writing, reading, or science lessons; the interest-led learning encompasses them all.

The process can be just as creative as it is educational. For example, if your child is interested in space like Trevor was, you can build space-themed LEGO projects, conduct experiments to understand meteor impacts on the moon, create models of the solar system, and watch educational videos. Similarly, if they are fascinated by American Girl dolls, you can delve into historical accuracy analysis, read related stories, and engage in various creative activities.

The key is to incorporate play, art, literature, and discussions related to your child's interests and ages. You can let them pretend to be astronauts, explorers, or historical figures and immerse themselves in the subject. This approach not only makes learning enjoyable, but also covers various subjects, including science, history, language arts, and even math.

The beauty of this approach lies in its flexibility. You don't have to stick to a rigid schedule or subject plan. If your children's interest wanes or they develop new ones, you can easily adapt and move on. If some essential subjects need attention, you can address them separately, keeping the process stress-free and engaging.

Transitioning Beyond the Home

I remember talking to my friend Danielle who had already graduated her only child. Her daughter Ella was an artist and had spent the bulk of her elementary and high school years pursuing art. As Ella was nearing the end of her homeschooling, and was preparing to apply to colleges, she realized she needed a couple of science classes. Because she planned to go to art school, she chose to double up and take two nonlab science classes, figuring she'd never want to take a lab science once she got to art school.

The Best Thing. . .

It's a flexible way of learning that suits my flexible mind!

—Gabe, 13

Ella graduated Danielle's homeschool, was accepted into all of the art schools she applied to, and chose her favorite, going away to school the following year. After two years, Danielle called to tell me that Ella had switched majors and was now planning to go to medical school. She had taken an art class focused on the human body, was fascinated by the diagrams of the body systems, and decided to take biology as an elective. It was the first lab she had taken in her life, and during the first class meeting, she realized there was a lot she didn't understand, so after class she went up to the professor, told him she had been homeschooled with plans to be an artist, and didn't know all of the terminology used in class, nor what all of the equipment was used for since she'd never had the occasion to be in a science lab before.

Because Danielle prioritized learning how to learn over prescribing what Ella should learn, her daughter wasn't afraid to ask questions, admit she didn't know something, or ask for help. Ella is now in medical school, and on track to be a pediatrician. When a child is given permission to make mistakes and follow their interests, and knows that it's okay to not know something, they thrive.

As homeschooling parents, our journey is a remarkable adventure filled with twists and turns, changing interests, deep dives, and rabbit trails followed. We all start with the same passion: nurturing our children's curiosity, encouraging them to explore, ask questions, and savor the joy of discovering new things. But as the years pass, something interesting happens. When our kids reach the middle and high school years, our thinking takes a new turn.

It's during these years that the joy we've found in homeschooling starts to shift. We transition from carefree explorers who treat the world as our classroom to anxious people seeking a more structured, safer approach. Suddenly, it's not just about embracing the journey; it's about preparing our children for life beyond high school. We find ourselves in uncharted territory, worried about academic rigor, transcript building, and the anticipation of what lies ahead.

This shift can be a bit challenging, especially for parents of differently wired children. These amazing kids often have unique learning styles and strengths, and their interests might not fit neatly into traditional educational boxes. In fact, many of them have experienced frustration and disconnection with the conventional system, which is why they chose homeschooling in the first place. We recognized the need for an education that caters to their specific needs and passions.

The beauty of interest-led homeschooling, particularly for neurodivergent children, is that it taps into their strengths. It empowers them to embrace their passions and talents wholeheartedly. This engagement keeps their enthusiasm for learning burning brightly. Unlike traditional education, where learning can sometimes feel detached from real-life applications, interest-led homeschooling helps students see the purpose and relevance in what they study, and this can continue into the high school years.

Remember, one crucial aspect of this journey is truly understanding our children. It's recognizing their unique strengths, learning styles, and the interests that ignite their hearts. This involves valuing their natural talents and passions throughout their education, not just up to ninth grade. Here's the magical part: when we do this, our kids naturally start valuing their own education. They see meaning and significance in their learning journey. It becomes more than a list of assignments and exams; it's a purposeful exploration of their interests.

As our children enter their teenage years, the need for planning and preparing their future becomes evident. This is where the idea of backward thinking comes into play. Instead of imposing a predetermined curriculum and expecting our children to fit into it, we start with their aspirations and interests, and we work backward. It's a customized approach that considers what they want to do in the future and positions them for success.

The Best Thing. . .

I love the extra free time I get to explore
what I love.

—Jackie, 11

For instance, let's say your child dreams of becoming a zookeeper. You can shape their high school years around animal studies. Initially, this might involve comprehensive unit studies and hands-on experience caring for animals at home. As your child's interests and goals become clearer, you can fine-tune their education accordingly. If college is on the horizon, you can research institutions with relevant programs and work backward to ensure they meet the entrance requirements.

Some subjects, like math, writing, and reading, usually remain non-negotiable in their education. These skills are the foundation, and they continue to be cultivated throughout their high school years. However, these subjects can be creatively integrated to align with their interests. Math, for instance, can involve calculations related to animal care, budgeting for a future business, or understanding statistical data in their chosen field.

Writing skills can be developed in various ways. If your child is passionate about animals, they can maintain a blog sharing their experiences, write research papers on wildlife, or contribute to publications related to their interests. Reading can also be tailored to their chosen path, with a focus on texts and materials that deepen their understanding of their field.

The ultimate goal is not just to follow their interests, but also to prepare them for the future, whether it's college or another path. It's a holistic approach that ensures they are well prepared academically while passionately pursuing their interests.

But what about those kiddos who are not entirely sure about their future direction or the need for college? In these cases, your role as a parent is to facilitate their exploration of various interests. This stage can be incredibly rewarding as you expose them to a range of subjects and activities. As they experiment and discover what excites them, you provide the freedom and space to dive deeper into their newfound passions.

For younger children who are still in the process of uncovering their interests, you can provide a well-rounded education that touches on various subjects. In addition to the core subjects, introduce them to a broader spectrum of knowledge, offering a taste of different fields. This approach allows them to explore and discover what resonates with them.

The flexibility of interest-led homeschooling means your child's education can evolve as their interests develop. It's a process of ongoing discovery and refinement, much like fine-tuning a musical instrument. As they grow older and become more certain about their aspirations, you can gradually tailor their education to align with their goals. This approach not only ensures they have the academic foundation they need, but also respects their individuality and evolving interests.

Of course, the path to self-discovery can be filled with twists and turns. It's perfectly normal for children to change their minds. This is a crucial lesson to impart – that they are not bound to a single path, and it's okay to explore different directions. Many adults change careers or majors multiple times in their lives, and our children should feel empowered to do the same. It's vital to instill the idea that there's no one-size-fits-all formula for a successful and fulfilling future. Success can take many forms, and there are various paths to happiness and achievement. This understanding can relieve the pressure and anxiety that often accompany the traditional educational model.

One of the most significant advantages of homeschooling through interest-led learning is the flexibility it offers. It allows your children to explore their passions and curiosities, nurturing their innate desire to learn. This approach embraces the idea that there are no limits to knowledge and no end to the possibilities.

Remember, though, as a parent, you're not alone on this journey. Your role as a facilitator and guide is crucial, but it's also a partnership with your child. Engage in meaningful conversations with them to understand their needs and goals. Encourage them to be active participants in shaping their education.

Identifying non-negotiables in your curriculum, such as the core subjects of math, writing, and reading, provides structure and ensures a solid educational foundation. However, it's equally important to find innovative ways to dive into their interests. Explore different learning opportunities, whether it's through community classes, online courses, or mentorships.

In this journey of interest-led homeschooling, the world becomes your classroom. Museums, libraries, local organizations, and online resources offer a wealth of knowledge waiting to be explored. And most importantly, remember that you're not just preparing your children for high school or college; you're nurturing them for life. Your guidance and support will equip them with skills and confidence.

The Best Thing. . .

I get more time to learn about the things
I love doing.

—Ruth, 14

The Power of Self-Direction

Back when Trevor was in ninth grade, we seemed to be bickering about every little thing. I was probably being a bit too controlling, and neither of us wanted him to go back to a regular school. I'd been reading *The Self-Driven Child: The Science and Sense of Giving Your Kids More Control Over Their Lives* by William Stixrud and Ned Johnson and *The Teenage Liberation Handbook: How to Quit School and Get a Real Life Education* by Grace Llewellyn at the time, and realized that Trevor needed to take a more active role in his own learning. He was spending time on things he didn't see as valuable and was fighting me every step of the way.

The idea behind the premise of kids taking on a more self-directed approach, especially in their teen years, is that school can feel like a waste for many kids and teens. Sure, our kids, especially our teens, can be impulsive, opinionated, and sometimes misguided, but they're also at home where they're loved, forgiven, nurtured, and given valuable lessons when they make mistakes. So, it can be empowering to let them customize their education to fit their interests and goals.

It's a compelling practice to give our kids this time to dive deep into their passions. It's a way for them to discover what truly excites them and how they might shape their future. I'm sure many of you have teens who'd rather binge-watch a show or play video games all day. Handing over the reins can be quite daunting, but bear with me. At the beginning of our first self-directed year, things were a bit rocky. Trevor was up and down, especially with math, which wasn't getting the attention it deserved. We made an agreement that he would manage his time better, and he did remarkably well. Meanwhile, he was getting deeply involved in a couple of interests.

One of these interests that really stood out was video editing, particularly special effects, compositing, and CGI. He started with free software and pushed it to the limit, creating some cool videos. However, he realized the limitations of free software, and for his 16th birthday, asked for a subscription to the Adobe Creative Suite, which includes After Effects, Photoshop, Premiere, Lightroom, and more. He started exploring 3D compositing, green screen work, color correction, and more. He did some projects for friends, adding muzzle flashes, smoke, and lightsabers to their videos. One of his favorites was creating a lightsaber effect for a company called Rumble Lab. It was his first paid freelance project. He's genuinely passionate about video editing, even though his siblings might find it boring or can't see it as a career path. But Trevor's interests are vast. He learned different aspects of editing, including 3D modeling, rendering, and color correction. He launched a freelance business, and still has clients he works with five years later.

Self-directed learning is an excellent strategy for kids who are self-motivated or are driven by passionate interests in specific areas. The amazing thing about kids who are allowed to follow their interests and direct their own learning is that they start to figure out their own areas of weakness. They want to succeed in their areas of passion, so they work hard to shore up where they're struggling. While Trevor was super passionate about video editing, he started to realize that he needed to improve his handwriting and writing skills, as well as his knowledge in subjects like English, history, and government since those were areas where he felt less confident. So, he worked on filling those gaps by incorporating an English class and exploring different resources to enhance his knowledge. We discussed whether or not taking quizzes and tests as part of the learning process was important to him. Standardized testing can be frustrating due to the limited right-or-wrong nature, and we believe that authentic learning comes from discussions and real-world applications. We aim for mastery of the content rather than just chasing grades, so he chose not to waste his time on tests and quizzes. Instead, he learned all he could about a topic before moving on.

My friend Mary – mom of six adult children, grandmother to fourteen, great grandmother to nine, and great-great grandmother to one – has been a source of inspiration to me for years. She started a writers group for aspiring children's writers when she was in her sixties, and invited me to join while I was pregnant with Trevor. She watched him grow up through all his ups and downs, enjoying him as he reminded her of her youngest son, Joe. Passionate, multipotential, impulsive, argumentative, and intensely curious, Joe has three children, is a nuclear physicist, plays guitar in a band that performs in bar gigs all over the West Coast, and blows incredible works of glass art in a studio he built in his backyard. These stories remind me that, despite the challenging moments, we are the best parents for our kids, and they have the potential to achieve amazing things. Trusting the process and nurturing their individuality is key.

What If My Child Isn't Interested in Anything?

It is incredible that your homeschooled kids have the awesome opportunity to choose what they want to learn when they're truly interested in a particular subject. But what do you do when your kids have a hard time picking something or simply say *they're not interested in anything*?

The Best Thing. . .

We love being free to pursue our own projects
the most! We are into making Hobbit cloaks to
sell and writing a quarterly newspaper for our
neighborhood right now.
> —Brothers Josh and Josiah, 10 and 12,
> respectively

It all starts with a tiny flicker of enjoyment, meaning, or curiosity. Once
your kids have that initial positive experience with a topic, they'll be eager
to explore it further. This positive experience can come from chatting with
a friend, watching an exciting movie or documentary, going on a fun field
trip, observing someone else having a blast with something, or trying out a
quick, hands-on activity.

Don't forget, you have the opportunity to expose your kids to various
subjects, places, ideas, and viewpoints. After all, it's like planting seeds – you
never know which one will grow into a lifelong passion.

At a recent speaking event, I shared a video of robots that had been
programmed to dance in an incredibly lifelike way. It was amazing how
the moves so accurately mimicked biological movement, and the audience
loved it. This initial fun introduction sparked the interest of a young girl
who had come to the talk with her parents. She had never tried robotics
or coding before, and had always been intimidated by the idea of tech.
She decided it was something she'd like to try and asked her parents to
buy a couple of kits for her upcoming homeschool year. She spent the
year steeped in those kits, moved on to simple coding sites like MIT's free
Scratch software, then asked to build a raspberry pi computer. She realized that technology wasn't as intimidating as she thought and found a
new interest.

Years ago, we belonged to a homeschool co-op that held different clubs
during the social hour after lunch. Once a month there was a game club
where the kids shared their favorite games. They took turns introducing the
games they brought and listened to others share theirs. Then, adults, teens,
and younger children all played the games they were interested in. My
teen had brought in the game *Schmovie*, which involves reading, decision-
making, and creative thinking. I played with a younger kiddo who couldn't
read very well, but really wanted to "play the game Trevor brought" because

he looked up to him. Later that afternoon, he showed me a notebook full of letters and short words. He'd been practicing so he could play more independently next time. He was motivated to learn because he saw his friends having fun playing a game his idol had brought, and wanted to join in.

That sweet boy found his own flicker. He saw a skill he wanted to develop and went for it. Sometimes, it happens like this, and it's exactly what we hope for in self-directed homeschooling. But in other cases, like the first example, parents or homeschooling guides can help ignite that spark. I started the conversation with a robot video and the kiddo's parents suggested robotics kits and online websites. While that girl could have said no, she decided to give it a try, and found a new interest and skill.

However, it's not just about being exposed to something or having fun with it. We've all had fun doing things we wouldn't do again. So what makes your kids go from *that was fun* to *I want to explore this further*?

It all comes down to a connection with their identity, or how this new interest fits into who they are and what they value. For instance, the girl who learned to enjoy robotics might have decided it was fun, but chooses not pursue it any further. On the other hand, she could see how her coding and robotics skills might help her connect with tech-savvy homeschooling friends or be useful in her future career.

On episode eighty-eight of the *Raising Lifelong Learners* podcast and in his book, *Understanding the Gifted Child From the Inside Out*, Dr. Jim Delisle tells the story of a student who helped him see how important meaningful self-direction can be for the success of bright kiddos. He says, "In our special needs classroom, there was a boy who initially seemed disengaged, not showing much interest in the curriculum. However, one day, everything changed. He was incredibly enthusiastic about maple sugaring and excitedly shared about an early morning encounter he'd had with a skunk. It was a breakthrough moment, highlighting the power of aligning education with a student's interests.

I had attempted various teaching methods to reach him before, but they all failed because I was approaching education from my perspective, my ideas. It wasn't until I stepped aside and allowed the student's interests to guide the way that we made progress. This boy had a life beyond the classroom; he was a twelve-year-old businessman, running his own maple sugar enterprise. Despite his reluctance to engage with math and spelling in my class, he demonstrated these skills effectively in his business.

The breakthrough came when we connected his schoolwork to his entrepreneurial endeavors. Almost overnight, his problematic behaviors ceased, and we enjoyed two productive years together. It was about understanding what he needed from his viewpoint. This process wasn't just intellectual; it was also deeply emotional." Taking a student's passions seriously and acknowledging what they value can significantly boost their self-esteem.

The Best Thing. . .

I love all the rabbit trails I can go down. Right
now I am creating my own Brazilian museum.
                                    —Braelyn, 12

It's important to recognize that the boundary between cognitive and emotional learning is not as distinct as it may seem. When children open a book, they immediately react to its content. Is this something I'm interested in? Do I see it as important? These are not just cognitive skills; they are emotional and affective. We must acknowledge and foster the connection between these two aspects of learning.

The social and emotional component of learning is an essential component that should never be overlooked. Cognitive learning alone doesn't hold much significance, and it's important for us as homeschooling parents to remember to tap into that. When you validate the ideas and passions of your kiddos, it transforms the entire conversation and ignites their motivation. All children are inherently motivated in some way; it's a matter of identifying what truly excites and engages them.

Parents, particularly those who have taken on the role of both parenting and homeschooling, often bear the weight of responsibility. It's easy to feel like you might negatively influence your child's development. However, if you approach it with love, validation, and a willingness to follow their lead, you're more likely to provide them with what they truly need. It may not always align with conventional academic expectations, but it can be highly effective in nurturing their growth.

Sometimes, homeschooling kids are motivated not just by fun, but also by feeling behind their peers. Maybe they saw a neighbor's kid from public school doing math worksheets they couldn't manage, and it sparked a desire to catch up. One of my kids recently came to me about this. They had been

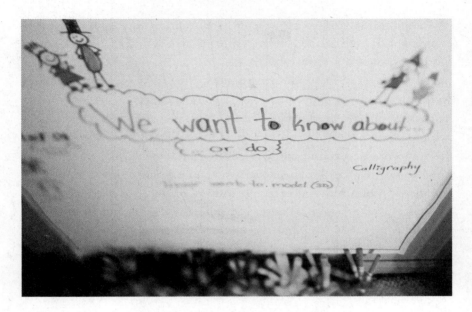

talking to a friend while that friend worked on their history homework and my kiddo worried they were way behind others their age. They aren't. In fact, this particular child is very bright, asynchronous, and several grade levels ahead in a number of areas as shown by a recent assessment they completed.

Instead of dismissing my child's worries, I asked for specifics on what was covered in their friend's work they didn't know. They rattled off the names of some battles, a war, and a few historic people they had not heard of before their friend read them the paper they'd been working on. We then talked about how they could find the answers to the questions they believed they couldn't answer. As we brainstormed, my kiddo realized that they weren't actually behind, and that they could read some of the history books we have around the house or watch a series of videos from the *Crash Course* YouTube channel. They're now crushing their way through European history videos and books, and will likely retain much more of that information than their friend, who is being told to learn the material to write a paper, then take a test on the material.

But even if your child decides to seriously explore a new interest, it can stall if they lack access to the necessary resources and opportunities. Think of a child who wants to create cool video effects but has no recording equipment or editing software, or someone who wants to learn German but has no one to practice with. Access to human, physical, financial, and digital resources, along with opportunities, time to work, classes, trips, or workshops is crucial in nurturing your child's interests.

Last, your child needs continued success in pursuing their interest. They need to see that they can make progress, even if there are challenges along the way. This success can start with small achievements, like reading their first letter or making a robot move. Over time, as they achieve more, their confidence grows. If they ever face an insurmountable obstacle for too long, perhaps due to a lack of resources or time, they might put their interest aside. However, they could always come back to it later or move on to something else. The key is to keep the journey enjoyable and filled with little successes to inspire their progress and watch for those flickers of interest so you can help fan them into flames of passion, interest, and learning.

Try This!

- **Tailor homeschooling to your child's interests and passions:** If your child loves animals, create a curriculum that revolves around zoology, including trips to the zoo, reading about animal behavior, and even fostering a pet or volunteering at an animal shelter.

- **Encourage curiosity and exploration:** Set up a "curiosity corner" in your home, where your child can explore various objects, books, and materials related to their interests.

- **Understand the power of passion-driven learning:** If your child is passionate about art, allow them to choose an art project they'd like to complete, and support them in acquiring the necessary supplies and skills.

- **Follow your child's lead:** If your child expresses interest in a specific historical figure, encourage them to research and create a presentation or a short play about that person's life.

- **Embrace neurodiversity:** If your child has sensory sensitivities, design a quiet and comfortable learning space with sensory-friendly tools like noise-canceling headphones or fidget toys.

- **Prioritize the development of self-directed learners:** Give your teenager more autonomy in choosing their learning materials and activities; then encourage them to create a personalized study schedule.

- **Let your child explore multiple interests:** If your child enjoys both science and art, help them combine these interests by creating scientific illustrations or conducting experiments related to artistic techniques.
- **Consider a backward-thinking approach:** If your child dreams of becoming a marine biologist, research college requirements for that field and work backward to create a high school plan.
- **Integrate essential subjects into your child's interests:** If your child is fascinated by cooking, use it as an opportunity to teach math (measuring ingredients), science (food chemistry), and reading (recipe comprehension).
- **Promote self-discovery and exploration:** Encourage your child to keep a journal where they document their daily experiences, interests, and ideas.
- **Offer a well-rounded education for younger children:** For a young child exploring interests, set aside specific days for various subjects, such as "Science Saturdays" or "Art Wednesdays."
- **Be flexible in your approach and adapt to changing interests:** If your child's interest in space shifts to marine biology, transition smoothly by finding marine biology resources, documentaries, and local aquarium visits.
- **Encourage your child to make mistakes and ask questions:** Celebrate mistakes as opportunities for learning and create a "Mistakes Board" where you document and discuss errors and their valuable lessons.
- **Empower your child to take control of their education:** Involve your child in setting their learning goals and milestones, allowing them to track their progress.
- **Connect education to your child's real-life interests and passions:** If your child is a sports enthusiast, incorporate sports statistics and history into math and history lessons.
- **Embrace the connection between cognitive and emotional learning:** When your child reads a book, discuss how the characters' emotions and experiences relate to their own.

4 | A Love of Learning

There is no such thing as a child who hates to read; there are only children who have not found the right book.

—Frank Serafini

A reader lives a thousand lives before he dies, said Jojen. The man who never reads lives only one.

—From *A Dance with Dragons* by George R.R. Martin

I first met Alice and her adorable daughter Jamie at a homeschool convention I'd been invited to speak at. Five-year-old Jamie was armed with some pocket money to spend. She seemed a bit unsure at first, contemplating her choices. Her initial instinct was to spend impulsively, but Alice gently advised her to think things over.

Finally, Jamie decided to use her money to buy the unabridged *Alice in Wonderland* novel. She disappeared under my display table as soon as she got back from making her purchase, creating her own cozy reading nook. By the end of the day, she had nearly devoured the entire book and finished it that night at home. Then, the next day, she returned with the rest of her money to purchase a study guide for *Alice in Wonderland*, which she promptly began working on in her secret little reading hideaway under my table.

It was in those moments that I truly fell in love with this remarkable child. Her enthusiasm for the novel and activity book was palpable as she completed the activities with a large purple marker clutched in her hand.

She tackled the study guide with fervor, answering questions in her large, childlike handwriting. It was charming!

Jamie loved to share her reading adventures and the details of what she was learning with anyone who stopped by our booth. She had these sweet little lists. And her unique way of explaining things was the best. What a treasure she was! This tiny sprite with a big book and even bigger words was a joy to watch.

Jamie reminds us that we don't have to follow a one-size-fits-all model. So many well-meaning relatives, friends, and acquaintances – non-homeschoolers – wonder how we fit all the things in, giving them separate attention like they do in a classroom. And, while, at first, new homeschoolers may stammer over the answer like I once did as I tried to explain to my father-in-law what we did all day, the longer we homeschool, the more confidently we're able to tell those questioners and naysayers that we don't! Homeschooling is not the same as sending our kids into a traditional classroom environment. It's not necessary to have a separate pre-designed curriculum for every subject and spread them all out over a six- to eight-hour time period.

The Best Thing. . .

Your brain can take the breaks it needs to learn all it can.

—Brenna, 11

Cultivating an environment where our kiddos feel safe to explore, experiment, and be themselves is truly the key. Letting them follow their passions, whether it's building with LEGOs, solving study guides, or diving into books, can lead to incredible outcomes. Jamie doesn't view learning as something confined to a rigid timeframe; she just learns because she loves to. If we can foster this approach with our kids, the world would undoubtedly be a much more amazing place.

What About Curriculum?

Asking a homeschooler about their curriculum is a bit like chatting about the weather with a stranger. It's a conversation starter when you find out someone homeschools their child, often driven by curiosity and the desire to avoid those awkward silences. It's the one word that seems to connect all homeschoolers – *curriculum*. However, for us, it's not that straightforward;

we're in the business of designing our own by picking and choosing what fits our family best. I encourage you to do the same.

When we first ventured into the world of homeschooling, I was terrified. The whole concept of homeschooling seemed like an imposing mountain, and I had a laundry list of worries. It didn't matter that I had taught in a classroom for more than a decade, was actively freelancing as an education and curriculum writer, or that my husband was still teaching. I fretted about how it might affect my relationship with my kids, how I'd manage to squeeze in my much-needed personal time, and whether I was equipped to teach the profoundly gifted, impulsive, and quirky child I had. The concerns about socialization danced in my head, but above all, it was the daunting task of picking the right curriculum.

The number of curriculum options out there is mind-boggling. It's like being at a buffet with countless dishes and not knowing where to start. I checked out websites of those well-known curriculum companies where you can order neatly packaged, grade-specific kits with everything you'd need for the year. These boxed curricula were enticing, offering the comfort of a structured safety net.

But here's the catch — my kiddo didn't quite fit into a neat grade-level box. He was asynchronous in his learning, excelling in one subject while being on par with his age in another. What he needed was a flexible curriculum that adapted to his interests and abilities rather than forcing him into a predetermined mold. Trying to make these adjustments within a boxed curriculum would have required loads of extra work, something I thought I could avoid by going the pre-packaged route.

It soon became clear that these boxed curricula weren't going to cut it for us. I realized I needed to roll up my sleeves, do some research, and piece together our own customized curriculum. Surprisingly, the process was far from the daunting task I'd imagined; it was actually a lot of fun.

Instead of trying to make lower-level courses fit, we could simply order programs and books tailored to my child's ability level. Recommendations from other parents in supportive groups led us to discover unique, engaging programs that aligned with his capabilities. This approach gave us the freedom to choose what we wanted to learn. Education was no longer about sticking to a rigid schedule; we could delve into subjects that genuinely interested us and set our own pace.

The best part for us? There was no pressure to adhere to a teacher's manual or a predetermined curriculum. Learning became a source of genuine excitement and discovery. We weren't confined to a one-size-fits-all program; we could explore different resources, switch things up, and adapt as needed. If something didn't work, we simply found an alternative – whether it was a writing program, a typing tool, a website, a video, or a new book.

The Best Thing. . .

The best part of homeschooling is that I get a say
in what I'm taught and how I get to learn it.
                              —Mason, 16

Of course, it did take some time and effort upfront to find these individual materials, but it was time well spent. Rather than searching for ways to supplement a traditional curriculum, we were investing in precisely what we needed. Sure, it could be a bit costly to gather resources from different places, but I'd rather invest in tools and materials that perfectly suited our requirements. And the idea that homeschoolers love the library? Absolutely true! We had the freedom to move forward when necessary and explore what challenged my child intellectually.

My friend Nikki has never been interested in pulling together her own curriculum or piecing together components from a variety of options. She prefers to have everything spelled out for her with options for a four-day- or a five-day-week. Her homeschool thrives when she can sit down on a weekend and fill out her and her kids' planners for the coming week. She marks off what each of her four children needs to do for each subject and creates checklists for them. She's able to pull all the resources each will need and pinpoint which lessons or activities will need her support, and where she can fit in time to manage the house.

Nikki is an organized soul with neurotypical kiddos who are an absolute delight to be around. They're well behaved and well adjusted. Our family loves them beyond bounds. I've often envied the ease in which Nikki seems to manage her homeschooling, and over the years, I've tried to emulate her from time to time.

And every time it's been a disaster. You see, Nikki's kids learn really well from books and workbooks. Sitting at a desk in their schoolroom helps them feel secure and gives them the structure they need to be successful. It's comforting to Nikki and her kids to have everything spelled out for them each day.

My kids need novelty integrated into their days. They need an overall idea of how the day will go and what outside activities we have planned, but they also need a lot of flexibility and room to perseverate if something feels interesting to them. They need to be able to do multiple lessons in a subject if they're on a roll, or permission to finish an entire week's worth of schoolwork on a Monday so they can take the rest of the week off to build the LEGO model they dreamed up.

Neither our family's nor Nikki's family's way of homeschooling is better. They're just different. If I tried to use a grade-level-based curriculum with my kids, none of us would follow through. If Nikki's family tried to piece things together and follow rabbit trails and changing interests, they'd feel overwhelmed and disorganized.

Crafting a Unique Learning Experience

The beauty of homeschooling is its flexibility, adaptability, and the freedom to craft a unique learning experience tailored to your family's needs.

Finding the right fit for your homeschooling journey may take some time, but it's well worth taking it. Homeschooling is all about creating an educational environment that's uniquely tailored to us, providing freedom, flexibility, and ease.

While there are plenty of online resources, video walk-throughs, blog posts, checklists, and cheat sheets to help you figure out what curriculum, style, or combination will work best for your family, ultimately, the best homeschool curriculum choice is the one you'll *use*. Too often we get caught up in the social media feeds or newsletter sales pitches and think we're missing out, or that our kids are. You can buy all the curriculum you can afford, but if it sits on the shelf in its shrink-wrap, it won't do you any good.

The Best Thing. . .

I like that we can do all sorts of science experiments.

—Braelyn, 12

Whether you choose to fully embrace one curriculum program, pick and choose pieces from several different companies; whether you follow a homeschool style in a flexible way, or abandon all structure altogether, homeschooling works. According to the National Home Education Research Institute (NHERI), homeschooling students tend to outperform their public school counterparts on standardized tests by a significant margin. On average, homeschoolers achieve scores in the range of 85% to 87%, whereas public school students typically score around 50%, and those scores are nondependent on the style of homeschooling a parent does or the curriculum a parent uses.

Homeschooling works because parents take a front-row seat to directing the path of their children's education, and most dedicated parents refuse to let their kids fail. There is nobody who will love a child more, advocate harder, or work more diligently to meet a child's needs than their parents. Homeschooling gives kids an edge because their parents are there creating the exact atmosphere their unique children need to thrive.

A Literature-Rich Home

A common denominator for success in education, regardless of your curriculum, schedule, or approach to learning, is cultivating a love of reading. It's no secret that having strong reading skills is a key factor in a child's success both during their early learning years and beyond. In fact, according to Cristy Whitten of Sam Houston State University in an article she wrote for the *Journal of Multidisciplinary Graduate Research* in 2016, a love of reading is the foundation on which other educational successes can be built. Regardless of curriculum choices, the schedule your family keeps, or the style of homeschooling you choose, cultivating a love of reading is the single best thing you can do to set your children up for future success. An easy first step is to create a literacy-rich environment in your home. A literature-rich environment helps your child develop solid literacy skills. It also fosters a genuine love for reading like sweet, young Jamie had.

A fantastic way to start is by ensuring that reading and writing materials are readily available. Keep them in plain sight and within easy reach, and your child will naturally gravitate toward them. Fill your living room shelves with a diverse array of books, including novels, picture books, atlases, and more.

Don't forget to subscribe to magazines and newspapers. Make sure there's a selection of age-appropriate books in your child's room, and keep notepads and writing tools, along with crayons and markers, in convenient places. You can even turn everyday items like signs, labels, and recipes into reading opportunities for your child.

Share your own love for reading and writing with your kids through everyday conversations. Children tend to mimic the behavior of the adults around them, so let them see you enjoying a good book or jotting down your thoughts regularly. It could be as simple as reading the paper while relaxing on a weekend morning, writing a note while they work on their schoolwork, or bringing a book to the beach or a picnic. Share your interests and your favorite childhood books with your child to create a special connection.

The Best Thing. . .

We can do basically whatever we want.

—Aberdeen, 9

Make a habit of reading together every single day. As Sarah Mackenzie wisely puts it in her book *The Read Aloud Family*:

When we read aloud, we give our kids practice living as heroes. Practice dealing with life-and-death situations, practice living with virtue, practice failing at virtue. As the characters in our favorite books struggle through hardship, we struggle with them. We consider whether we would be as brave, as bold, as fully human as our favorite heroes. And then we grasp—on a deeper, more meaningful level—the story we are living ourselves as well as the kind of character we will become as that story unfolds.

Reading together opens doors to independent learning and exploration, no matter whether it's a traditional book, a graphic novel, nonfiction, or historical fiction. What truly matters is the time you spend diving into these stories.

Reading aloud can also spark valuable conversations that help your child navigate the world's challenges. It might even lead to discussions you didn't anticipate. For instance, if your child is dealing with anxiety and worry, a well-chosen picture book on the topic could provide an opportunity for them to share their concerns.

Remember, reading aloud checks all the boxes in terms of social, emotional, and mental health. Sharing your love of reading with your child is a profound expression of love and a valuable tool for helping them navigate life.

Devoting regular time to reading with your child is a significant step in creating a literacy-rich home, and it's a wonderful way to bond with your little one. Studies show that children who are read to at least three times a week by a family member are almost twice as likely to excel in reading. Aiming for 20 minutes of reading a day can expose your child to a staggering 1.8 million words in a year! Bedtime is a perfect time to make this a daily practice, and it also promotes better sleep by avoiding screen time before bed. And, as homeschooling parents, we can easily incorporate reading throughout the day in small bursts. Can you imagine how many words your child will be exposed to by the time you graduate them?

Another way to infuse your home with literacy is through word games. Games like Scrabble, Boggle, Scattergories, Catchphrase, and Bananagrams are not only loads of fun, but also subtly teach important lessons about word structure and vocabulary. They're a fantastic addition to your family's game collection.

No literature-rich homeschool is complete without regular visits to the library. There's no better place to ignite a love for the written word. Make trips to your local library a regular family event, taking advantage of child-focused programs like story times, crafts, and learning groups. These outings also give your child the chance to discover fresh reading material that aligns with their interests. Consider keeping a "library bag" in your living room or another common area to keep your child's selected books organized and easily accessible.

With a bit of planning and creativity, your home can be transformed into a literacy-rich haven, helping your child develop essential reading and writing skills while sharing countless enjoyable moments.

The Best Thing. . .

If you're sick you don't have to miss school and you get lots of breaks and you get to see your family all the time.

—Blythe, 6

Simplifying to Foster a Climate of Learning

One of the hardest things about homeschooling is the feeling that we can never do enough. I've been there, juggling the rat race and feeling like I'm dropping the ball. But I've discovered that simplifying my homeschool day can make a world of difference. And by *simplify*, I don't mean sacrificing all the fun or the important subjects. It's all about shifting the focus from quantity to quality to bring clarity and calm into our homeschooling journey.

Shortly after my oldest was born, I read a passage in a parenting book I'll always remember. The passage described the overwhelming anxiety new parents face, suggesting invaluable advice. It advised readers to focus on accomplishing one thing each day, other than taking care of the baby, and considering that a win. At first, I thought, "One thing? That can't possibly be enough. There are so many things to do while I'm home on maternity leave." I was confident I could do more, maybe even do it all while caring for a newborn. And I did . . . for a while. It wasn't long before I began to struggle. I was overwhelmed, exhausted, and burnt out.

Trevor was different from the beginning. He was opposite of just about every description of ages and stages in every book I read. He didn't sleep. He nursed around the clock. He was unusually alert and vocal. He needed me constantly. Sure, there were joyful moments, but some days, that joy was hard to find.

There are countless ways to homeschool, and that's one of the beautiful aspects of teaching at home. I'm grateful there's no one-size-fits-all approach. But, much like being a new parent, homeschooling can feel daunting. We're faced with numerous decisions, and then we must put those choices into action. As a homeschooler, it's important to remember you don't have to cover every subject every single day. To set yourself up for success and make your homeschool day manageable, try to simplify by focusing on your top priorities – your *must-dos*.

So, what exactly are these *must-dos* all about? They're the main things your homeschooler wants or needs to do on any given day, like the *one thing* of Trevor's babyhood, that will allow you to consider your homeschool a win for the day. Your *must-dos* can change daily or remain the same. For us, math is a daily constant, and my homeschoolers' *must-dos* always include some form of reading and writing as well, though the way they practice those skills may vary.

Can we do more than those three things? Of course, and there are days when we do much, much more. One of the great things about homeschooling is that we don't have to rush or cram every moment with tasks. By honing in on just a few things each day, my children have plenty of time to explore their interests and dive into their passions.

It all comes down to our *why*. I homeschool so my kids can pursue their interests and learn at their own pace. I want them to be able to accelerate in areas of strength and slow down in areas where they struggle. I want them to enjoy the process of learning and cultivate a lifelong love of learning within them. When we try to cover every subject daily, our time together feels rushed. I work from home, my kids want to play, engage in other activities, finish their chores, and simply have downtime. They want to enjoy their friends and make it to outside activities. Rushing through the day can turn learning into a chore, and that's not what I want.

The Best Thing. . .

When I don't understand something Mommy comes to help me.

—Hyacinth, 7

I recently heard an interview where one of my favorite authors, Kim John Payne, from *Simplicity Parenting*, was discussing what he called "the undeclared war on childhood." Kim discussed the idea that kids are pushed to grow up too fast, then end up stressed and overwhelmed. He shared experiences from his practice where children, overwhelmed by stress, were able to finally relax and allow their true gifts to shine through. He likened stressed-out ten-year-olds and burnt-out fifteen-year-olds to children in war-torn countries suffering from PTSD. This drives home the importance of simplifying and reducing the pressure.

Simplifying our homeschool helps to foster a climate that is more conducive to learning. It prepares kids for the future by allowing them time to focus on their passions. Returning to a simpler way of life doesn't mean we're hindering our children's potential. Kim firmly believes that

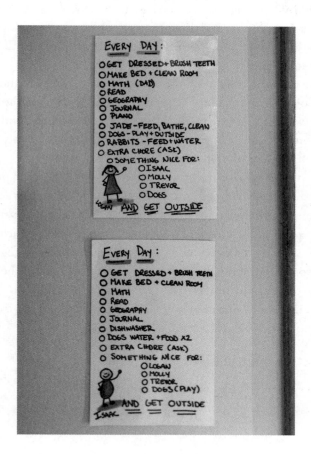

over-scheduling children doesn't give them a head start; it holds them back. The future belongs to creative entrepreneurs, those who create their own environments, and this creativity emerges through play and imagination, not through every moment being scheduled. We're setting the stage for their futures when we lead by example.

By simplifying to create a climate of learning, and focusing on those *must-dos*, our kids will have plenty of time to engage in learning, exploring their interests, and answering their countless questions. And without fail, when the learning time is over, your kiddos will still be brimming with interest and energy to continue exploring independently.

I'm not a therapist like Kim John Payne, nor have I conducted extensive research with thousands of kids, but I've been there. I was a stressed out sixteen-year-old with profound anxiety and I entered college as a burnt out eighteen-year-old. I have struggled with bouts of depression and insomnia. I want better for my kids, and I know you want better for yours. Homeschooling is a powerful advantage we can leverage to create the life that we want, the educational experience our kids need, and the childhood they deserve.

Try This!

- **Embrace asynchrony:** Recognize if your child excels in some subjects while being on par with their age in others, and adapt the curriculum accordingly.
- **Prioritize flexibility:** Give your child the freedom to set their own pace and explore subjects that genuinely interest them.
- **Harness the library:** Incorporate library visits into your routine, allowing your child to discover new reading materials and resources.
- **Focus on must-dos:** Prioritize subjects that are essential for your child's development, but remember that you don't have to cover every subject daily.
- **Be a reading role model:** Let your child see you enjoying books, magazines, or writing in everyday situations.
- **Make reading together a habit:** Set aside dedicated time for shared reading, encouraging independent exploration of various book genres.
- **Infuse literacy into daily life:** Encourage your child to read signs, labels, and recipes as part of daily life.

- **Word games for learning:** Play games like Scrabble, Boggle, or Bananagrams to make learning fun and engaging.
- **Allow room for play:** Provide downtime for your children to explore their interests and indulge in imaginative activities.
- **Support mental health:** Encourage open conversations and provide resources to help them navigate challenges and stress.

5 | Play Matters

Play is our brain's favorite way of learning.

—Diane Ackerman

Tess gave herself over completely to the game and the joy of companion-ship. It happened occasionally that she met a friend of a sort in the animal world, but as with human friends, it always seemed to be hard work. This was different. The chipmunk was as eager for company as she was.

—From *Switchers* by Kate Thompson

Jacob's stuffed animals have been a significant part of his homeschooling journey, even now that he's a teenager. They've played a unique role in helping him process challenging topics. Whenever he delves into subjects like slavery, wars, or situations where people are treated unfairly, his anxiety spikes and his sense of justice is aroused, so he gathers his stuffed animal crew around. It's their way of joining him on this learning adventure.

When he's grappling with a particularly tough topic, these stuffed animals become his partners in reenactment. His mom, Sarah, says it's incredible to see how this imaginative play helps him make sense of complex subjects. She says it all goes back to the valuable lessons he learned when they joined The Learners Lab, my community for families homeschooling outside-the-box kiddos.

Sarah vividly remembered the games challenge one month, where the kids were encouraged to incorporate games into various subjects for a week. Jacob, while brilliant in many ways, has always had a challenging time with games, especially when he loses. Sarah remembered reading in the parent forum that it's often the child who struggles with games who needs them the most. Those insights were a game-changer for them.

Role-playing with his stuffed animals the act of being a sore winner or loser as well as a good winner or loser was eye-opening. It taught Jacob valuable lessons about sportsmanship and resilience. Because of this, they've begun incorporating games into their learning routine every day. These days, games are an integral part of Jacob's homeschooling, whether they're related to his study topics or just for the pure fun of it. They even sneak in some learning during vacation breaks with games.

Playful humor is another constant in Sarah and Jacob's homeschool. They use both English and Spanish in their lessons, and some of the stuffed animals are "fluent" in only one language. This sometimes leads to amusing cases of "lost in translation." But, laughter has become a crucial part of their learning journey, and these language mix-ups just add to the fun and uniqueness of their homeschooling experience.

The Purpose of Play

Play is a fundamental aspect of human life. It's found in every culture and all throughout time. From the giggles of children on a playground to the strategic moves of chess players, play takes on so many different forms and serves countless purposes. But what exactly is play? Is it merely a frivolous pursuit or does it have deeper meaning?

Stuart Brown, author of *Play: How It Shapes the Brain, Opens the Imagination, and Invigorates the Soul* and founder of the National Institute for Play, has dedicated his career to understanding the mysteries of play. He believes that play is not just something kids do, but a biological and psychological need for everyone, no matter their age. In his extensive research, Brown defines *play* as any voluntary activity that is pleasurable, spontaneous, and purposeless. This definition covers the entire spectrum of play-like activities, from the antics of kids to the playful pursuit of strategy games played by teens and adults. Brown emphasizes that play not only brings joy, but is an incredible stress-reduction tool.

The Best Thing. . .

We can go places on the weekdays so we can
have a better time because places are so full on
the weekends.

—Aberdeen, 9

Psychologist Peter Gray also talks frequently about the importance of play for children. In his book, *Free to Learn: Why Unleashing the Instinct to Play Will Make Our Children Happier, More Self-Reliant, and Better Students for Life* he argues that free play, where children engage in activities without adult intervention, is a cornerstone of their growth and development. Gray's research contends that when kids are given the autonomy to engage in self-directed play, they gain vital life skills, including problem-solving, decision-making, and conflict resolution. Furthermore, play fosters emotional intelligence as kids navigate social interactions and learn to regulate their emotions.

My kids are very dramatic. Not surprising since they've all been involved in theater at one time or another during their lives, and one plans to pursue a BFA in performance once she graduates high school. It's to be expected, then, that their play tends toward reenactments, role-play, and scene creation. They love to imagine, and often act out long, dramatic scenes in the yard.

When my oldest was about twelve, he created a game called *Dramatic Deaths*. Dramatic Deaths soon became the hit of the neighborhood, with my kids, who were twelve, eight, six, and two at the time, and a bevy of children — tots through teens — from all around the city dropping over to play. My son would drag out the foam and Nerf swords and guns, and the kids would divide them up, then work to prompt the most dramatic deaths as possible from each other.

My kids grew to be so adept at dying, that I had to banish the game to the backyard because it was disconcerting for passersby to watch a two-year-old die by asphyxiation and collapse into a limp heap on the side of a suburban road while other children looked on, clapping. We had more than one car stop to see if the kids needed help. The backyard was a better place to stage dramatic fake deaths. The game went on for a while, gaining so much popularity that we met more of our neighbors than we would have otherwise. In fact, the kids loved it so much that they brought it to a homeschool playgroup we'd recently joined.

The playgroup seemed like it was going to be a great fit for our family. We'd meet once a week with the same families, sometimes for field trips, and other times for unstructured play dates at local playgrounds. Unstructured play with a group of kids of varying ages my kids could grow with was an ideal homeschool group, in my opinion, as I could take care of the academics, but wanted them to have regular time to develop friendships. As expected, the other kids at the playground meetups loved Dramatic Deaths. It fit the perfect definition of *play*, as Peter Gray describes it.

Child-Directed Play

Gray says play doesn't fit neatly into a single box. Instead, it's a mix of different traits to varying degrees. Gray says:

- Play is self-chosen and self-directed.
- Play is intrinsically motivated – means are more valued than ends.
- Play is guided by mental rules, but the rules leave room for creativity.
- Play is imaginative.
- Play is conducted in an alert, active, but relatively nonstressed frame of mind.

Dramatic Deaths was popular with kids of all ages because they chose and created it. The outcome changed each time so they were motivated to play again and again. There was a simple implied rule to "out-die" each other, but tons of flexibility within the game to be creative. It was steeped in the imagination of the kids – from the littlest to the teens. There was no stress, and lots of action.

The Best Thing. . .

While everyone is at school, we can go to fun
spots that aren't too crowded.

—Ainsley, 12

There's a problem, though, as Gray says, "Since about 1955 . . . children's free play has been continually declining, at least partly because adults have exerted ever-increasing control over children's activities." He goes on to say that a big part of the issue is parents hovering and interfering with their children's play. Homeschooling parents can be just as guilty of this as any parent. A few weeks into Trevor's game being played at our homeschool group meetups, the organizer asked him not to play it anymore. She said it was making a few of the parents uncomfortable.

So, he tried. Over the course of the next two weeks, he tried to steer the play to another game, but the kids wanted to play Dramatic Deaths whenever they saw him. He stopped playing and hung out by me or played with the babies, but the majority of the kids played on. They loved the game because play, when self-directed and originating from children themselves, is where they learn essential skills and feel confident. It's all about kids taking the lead and guiding their own activities. They were in charge and kept playing because they loved having that role.

Eventually, the organizer suggested that it might be better if our family stopped coming to playground days for a while so the rest of the kids had time to be introduced to *more appropriate and structured games*. They forgot that real magic happens when play is driven by kids, not adults. And we realized that the group wasn't a fit for us after all.

Allowing children to take the reins in their play sets the stage for mental well-being, among other benefits. It's all about giving them the space and freedom to shape their own play experiences, which builds a strong foundation for their future mental health. So, creating space for self-directed play is a wonderful gift to offer our children.

Play is an opportunity for kids to explore and nurture their unique self-identified passions. When they decide what games or activities they want to engage in during free play, they're experiencing a chance to be self-directed learners. It's about them taking the lead, pursuing their interests, and letting their imaginations roam free. They will benefit from these skills for the rest of their life. Take Dramatic Deaths, for example: the game that upset a group of homeschooling parents who preferred to direct their children's play in calm, structured activities inspired Trevor to audition for a staged play version of H.G. Well's *War of the Worlds* when he saw a notice that it was coming to a local community theater.

Trevor knew that only the two lead actors in the play survived, and all others would die throughout the play. He also noted on the audition form that ensemble members would play multiple roles since each scene ended in deaths. He wrote on his form that he only wanted to accept an ensemble role as one of his best skills was dying, and he'd like a part that allowed him

to die in as many ways as possible. He was cast in the ensemble and died spectacularly over the course of the two-hour show — by asphyxiation, ray gun, hanging, decapitation, and more. His free play had paid off, and it led to him auditioning for several play adaptations of favorite books, novels, and court cases over his middle school and high school years.

Traditional settings like school or organized sports come with external motivators like grades, praise, or trophies. With free play, it's all about what children genuinely want to do. The learning and personal growth that naturally follows are bonuses, *not* the main purpose of the activity. So, as parents, we can encourage this kind of play and let it work its magic in our kiddos' lives.

Emotional Resilience Through Play

Play is where children take their first steps into decision-making, problem-solving, self-control, and rule-following. When kids guide their own free play and tackle the challenges that arise, they learn to exercise self-discipline. They need to control their behavior and follow the rules to be part of the group. As children navigate their physical and social surroundings through play, they start to feel a sense of security in the world. This is the aspect of play that brings the most psychological benefits. It helps to protect kids from anxiety and depression.

Gray and Stuart both believe that kids who don't get to shape their own actions, make decisions, solve problems, and learn to follow rules during play may grow up feeling they have no control over their lives and future. They might believe their future is left to chance and the benevolence of others. Kids who believe they have a say in their own future are less likely to struggle with anxiety or depression compared to those who feel they have no control. Gray suggests that the lessons learned during playtime serve a critical role in supporting our mental well-being.

The Best Thing. . .

Instead of being told what to do like I would at school, I like that I can choose what to do. If I ever want to, I can stop and do something fun. And I don't have to stay in class for seven hours.

—Harper, 15

Children learn to control their emotions, even complex ones like anger and fear, through play. During play, children willingly put themselves in situations that are both physically and socially challenging. They learn the skill of controlling their emotions in these situations. They learn that these activities are most pleasurable when they are just a little bit spine-tingling, whether it be through imaginative role-playing or dangerous exploits like swinging, sliding, or climbing trees. For each youngster, "the right dose" differs, as Gray puts it.

The development of anxiety disorders can be significantly influenced by one's capacity to control emotions, which is something that is learned through play. Gray points out that people with anxiety disorders frequently worry about losing control over their emotions, which makes them uneasy about their own fear. Because of their anxiety over losing emotional control, even circumstances that cause only a little anxiety might cause a great deal of panic. However, engaging in activities like dancing or singing can be a terrific way to decompress. Your body produces endorphins, which help you feel good, when you are having fun and laughing with others.

Adults who didn't have the chance to encounter and deal with emotionally difficult play scenarios are more prone to feel worried and overwhelmed. Therefore, as parents, we may encourage play activities that build our kids' emotional fortitude and prepare them for the trials of life.

Children learn how to get along with one another as equals and establish friends via play. Making new friends and learning how to treat one another fairly comes naturally through social play. Children learn to be aware of the wants of their peers and make an effort to address those needs in order to maintain the play because play is voluntary and playmates may leave the game at any point if they feel uncomfortable.

Gray believes that the most important evolutionary role of human social play is learning how to get along and work with others on an equal footing, and that social play is how nature teaches young people they are not unique. Even kiddos who are good at games and play must treat the wants and needs of the other as equal to their own or they risk being excluded by those they want to play with. The loss in play may be a cause of the culture's developing social isolation and sense of loneliness, according to Gray, who also notes that it may be a potential precursor to mental health issues.

The main benefit of play is that it makes people happy. When asked what makes them happy, children consistently report that playing with friends is the most joyful activity for them. Gray further believes that, as a society, we have come to the conclusion that, in order to keep kids safe and educate them, we must take away their favorite activities and keep them in settings where they are constantly monitored and evaluated by adults.

The Best Thing. . .

When I'm done with the things I have to do
every day, I like having a lot of free time. I like
being able to finish my work whenever I want,
so I don't have to wait for anyone else to be done
before I can play.

—Rowan, 7

Although it may be difficult to define, *play* is simply the pursuit of delight and pleasure through varied activities. The thread that runs through every area of human existence, tying together generations, civilizations, and different facets of our lives, is play. It serves as a classroom for kids, an escape for adults, a breeding ground for creativity, and the link that holds us all together. Let's not overlook the value of play, the source of our most price-less and treasured moments of joy as we journey through life.

Play-Based Learning

Kim recalls that one of her favorite memories of her homeschooling years, even after almost sixteen years in the trenches, was when her oldest kiddo Jackson was six or seven. He was fascinated with animals, particularly with the black bear, and begged to watch documentaries over and over again about their habits. Kim cuddled on the couch with Jackson and his little sister Jess, watching animated shows, documentaries, nature series episodes, and YouTube shorts about black bears and then reading books, magazines, and websites about them, too.

It wasn't enough for Jackson, though. He built forest habitats out of blocks for the black bear figurines Kim had ordered online. He built scenes and more forests out of LEGO bricks, and painted with construction paper and on old cardboard boxes salvaged from the recycle bin. He created a kid-sized habitat in the corner of the family room where he and Jess pretended to be black bears. When friends came over, they joined in too, either becoming other animals in the forest or bears themselves.

Some days, Jackson pretended to be a bear scientist, studying them in their natural habitat, or a nature photographer, out to get the shot with the camera he made from cardboard. He and Jess wanted to eat blueberries for their snacks because that was something black bears enjoyed eating. Jackson and Jess played and learned about black bears for weeks and weeks that year. Kim says that they still remember more about black bears than any other animal they studied in all the years of homeschooling together.

Play-based learning is powerful.

Tina, a veteran homeschool mama of three, told me once that, in her opinion, the greatest advantage to homeschooling has been having time to play. She went on to tell me that when her kids were younger, she could let them explore, play, ramble, and do what they wanted. Her role in those early years was to give them words to identify what they were doing and to express how they were feeling. As they grew older, she facilitated more of their learning through imaginative play, role-play, and more. She said, though, that what she loved best about their time together homeschooling was that the kids were able to keep playing through their teen years, and now her adult children look forward to the holidays and weekends they can stop over to have "family game night."

It's important to remember that play in the early years sparks the beginning of the learning journey like we saw with Jackson and Jess when they remembered their black bear facts years later. We can take heart and know that the payoff is worth it, and no "play breaks" will be wasted time when we think about Tina's adult children coming home for game nights once they moved out. Integrating play into our homeschool can teach us that play is more than just fun; it's a lifetime of relationship-building, growth, and discovery.

Your play-based learning journey begins when you bring your tiny bundles of wonder home. In the precious first year of life, play is all about sensory experiences. Everything seems to find its way to your kiddos' mouths, from soft rattles to teething rings. The sheer joy of reaching for a dangling mobile becomes cause for fascination and excitement. Peek-a-boo inspires those first smiles, and the world starts to unveil its magical secrets.

As your little ones take their first steps into the world of play, their imagination starts to shine. Building blocks, colorful crayons, and dolls become the tools of their creativity. Tea parties with stuffed animals and superhero capes transform them into world-savers, nurturers, and explorers. Between the ages of two and five, "Look at me!" becomes their mantra as they discover their own abilities.

The elementary years usher in a whirlwind of active play. The backyard echoes with laughter as children run, jump, and explore the nuances of building friendships. It's soccer games or theater performances on weekends, tree-climbing adventures, and endless board games and puzzles. Building model cars, crafting intricate LEGO worlds, and experimenting with structured activities like music lessons, karate, community theater, sports camps, and more fill their days with excitement.

The Best Thing. . .

> I feel like I'm getting a better education because I
> can do stuff that's up my alley.
> —Lincoln, 12

The teenage years bring a new dimension to play. Your kids are discovering who they are, and exploring the social and intellectual parts of themselves. Teens become more inclined toward group activities, joining sports teams or clubs. Theater rehearsals, debate competitions, forming rock bands, and football games on Friday nights become part of their world. Play extends to movie nights with friends, experimenting with artistic expressions through writing, painting, and even video games. The teen years can be some of the best times, especially if you make your home the place to be. Stock up on snacks, soda, and create a place to hang out and play or watch movies, and their friends will want to be at your house. We have a partially finished basement, and over the last few years we've give a "family gift" for the holidays to add to the space. We now have one of those arcade basketball games, exercise equipment, a small ping pong table, and an older television hooked up to streaming services with a comfy futon couch to watch from. I keep an air pop popcorn maker and a bunch of flavored popcorn salts, and the teens come over and hang out. When you create a safe, but fun, place where teens can be themselves, they'll want to be around, and your relationship with your own kids will grow stronger.

Your kids' play journey doesn't end once they head off to college, get a job, or just begin their adulthood while staying home. Between the ages of eighteen and twenty-nine, play intersects the responsibilities of work and education. College life becomes one big adventure, a world of both learning and social discovery. Those who don't go to college are playing around to figure things out in their own way and time. My oldest is twenty-one at the time I'm writing this, and is sitting in our kitchen with a couple of friends playing Catan and talking about their day. One of those young men is working full-time while taking college classes on the side. One is a full-time firefighter and EMT. My son took a few classes at the local college, decided that formal education wasn't for him, and has several different jobs. He is a freelance audio and video editor, is a photographer, shoots and edits footage for a YouTube channel focused on race cars and the three friends who own them, just finished teaching a class on special effects to a group of teens at a local film school, and is working toward both his FAA Part 107 Drone License and his real estate license. Young adults explore passions like Trevor is doing. They go hiking, painting, and play musical instruments. The concept of play blends with self-exploration, and every day offers opportunities to create lasting memories.

The need to play doesn't end just because we grow up, though! Work becomes a significant part of adult life, but so does the need for leisure. Hobbies like gardening, book clubs, and cozy evenings with a movie provide a much-needed break from the demands of daily life. The challenge lies in maintaining that essential work-play balance for overall well-being.

Play remains vital as our kids grow and move out, and we age. Gentle exercises like yoga or tai chi help maintain mobility and balance. Community activities, volunteering, and quality time with grandchildren become sources of joy. Logic puzzles and games offer mental stimulation, and life experiences continue to provide opportunities for play, exploration, and connection. And, if we've done our jobs well, our kids, then theirs, will want to come back home to play.

In the story of life, play is an ever-constant – and much-needed – companion, adapting to our changing needs and desires. It's a joyful journey, a lifelong source of growth, connection, and delight. Our role, as parents, is to nurture this essential aspect of our children's lives, guiding them and providing the tools they need to thrive at each stage.

The Best Thing. . .

I liked it because I've had problems since I was
a child, and homeschooling gave me the chance
to learn at my own pace and the full attention
I needed to do well. Family and friends were
always there for me, and I always knew I could do
great things.

—Taylor, 22

When we embrace every phase of play, and savor the beauty it brings to our lives, we remember that life is an adventure. Living it well starts at home, and homeschooling allows us to add play in as often as possible.

Gameschooling

One of the easiest way to add play into your day is to use games to do some of the academic lifting for you, and gameschool! Simply put, gameschooling is using gameplay as a teaching tool with kids of all ages. Games can be used to teach a variety of skills, including math, social and emotional learning, problem-solving, and anger management.

Isaac did not like using his imagination until we started playing Dixit as a family. He's a very logical-thinking kiddo, and sees things in a very black-and-white way, so noticing art, inferring meaning, or spinning stories has always been tougher for him than a subject like math. In the game of Dixit, one player is the storyteller, and on his turn he looks at the cards in his hand and makes up a sentence or phrase about one of them. The sentence should be inspired by the art on the card. Then, the other players look at their cards and choose the one that they think most closely represents the storyteller's sentence. All players give their card to the storyteller face down, and the storyteller mixes them all up with their card, and randomly places them face-up on the table. Players must decide which card is the storyteller's original card. Art, creativity, strategy, active listening, thinking, and communication skills are all a part of the game as players try to out-score one another and race their rabbits across the board. Dixit is Isaac's favorite game, and since we started playing a few years ago, we've added multiple expansion decks to our collection.

Homeschooling parents have the opportunity to change their educational approach to better suit their unconventional learners thanks to game-schooling. While some kiddos love it simply because it gives them the chance to study subjects they previously couldn't, others just prefer learning with games. When children can pursue their personal interests while learning, especially in a gaming environment, they become intrinsically motivated to engage in the process. Kids are eager to play and often aren't aware that they are learning, so they require fewer reminders and redirections.

There are so many benefits to gameschooling, and you can find subject-based game lists and suggestions online at HomeschoolAdvantage. Resources. Each kiddo is unique, but all can benefit from the power of play!

Through game-based learning, students can develop their critical, creative, and problem-solving thinking skills. Many games provide recurring logic and creativity challenges, giving kids a safe environment to hone their judgment, decision-making, and quick-thinking abilities.

The development of children's interpersonal skills, such as cooperation, sharing, and effective communication, is also crucial. Playing games cultivates characteristics like patience and the ability to take turns, and these abilities naturally transfer to relationships outside of game contexts.

Children who are interested in a subject tend to learn knowledge more quickly and to engage with it more thoroughly. Games have the power to bring life to once tedious subjects, transforming them into interesting learning opportunities and making it easier for teachers to impart knowledge.

Games have a unique ability to present novel and alternate perspectives on difficult themes. They might provide the information in a way that more successfully connects with the pupils, promoting a deeper comprehension of the subject.

A special bond is created when playing games together around the living room or kitchen table. Playing games brings your family closer together. While the repetition of games helps to solidify learning concepts, multiplayer games encourage relationships and teamwork among participants.

Overall, gameschooling creates a setting that encourages children to follow their interests and develops self-assured, original thinkers. While having a blast playing games, kids actively participate in their own learning journeys.

There are a ton of games and hobbies to pick from in the world. This is perfect since it's crucial to have a variety of options available because even a favorite game can get dull after a time. To study language arts topics, for example, you could play Pictionary. You can search especially for games that accomplish a learning aim. Spelling may be improved using Scrabble. Prime Climb is a fantastic game for teaching multiplication, and I adore 24 for teaching math problems that require more than one step. You may choose games that suit your family's needs and educational objectives by being aware of the various types of games that are out there. Board games, video games, and card games are the three main categories of games. They each have benefits.

The Best Thing. . .

I really enjoy the time I spend with my family and getting to know each of them better. I'm excited to learn about a lot of things, and I get to learn what I want to. When I ask "why," I get a reason, and I learn how something helps me. It's become clear to me that I'm good at art. In this area, I can spend a lot of time getting better and better. I like to read books, write stories, and work on other cool things too. I love having more time to do things I enjoy.

—Bella, 14

Board games are a classic way to use games in learning. When you were young, playing board games like Candy Land would have helped you learn your colors, shapes, and how to count. Board games come in a wide variety of genres. Teamwork skills are taught through cooperative games. Instead of competing against one another, players cooperate to achieve a common objective in these board games. These cooperative games help kids learn how to compromise, communicate, and share for the benefit of the group. They also promote collaboration. You might be able to locate a board game that has been altered to fit a particular theme if your child has a favorite character or television program. Games with a competitive or strategic element can instruct in social skills, academic content, or even executive function skills.

Both inside and outside of homeschooling communities, there is constant debate over video games. Parents worry that their children may become overly dependent on technology, despite the fact that it can be a terrific learning tool because it is so adaptive and can personalize the experience for your child. However, it's crucial that we provide our children with the means to develop self-control. We must teach our children how to use video games, apps, and the internet responsibly while they are still at home since these things are here to stay. Video games come in a variety of forms, such as app-based, simulation, role-playing, and story-based games. Kids' brains are engaged when playing video games to come up with a step-by-step solution to the issue.

Set boundaries that make you feel safer if including screen time makes you uneasy. Set time restrictions, only permit games that are directly related to a lesson, or better, whenever possible, participate in the game experience. You might wish to experiment with including video games as breaks in your homeschooling schedule or allow kids to play after school or on weekends.

Cards are easy to add into your homeschooling repertoire. A regular 52-card deck may be used to play countless card games, making them incredibly flexible. Memory, color identification, and pattern skills can all be taught through these games. The guidelines for several card games are available online. In the event that you don't have any cards, there are also printable solutions.

There are so many unusual varieties of card decks available. SET is a favorite in our family. We always carry a deck of SET cards with us when we go out because we enjoy using our visual-spatial skills to pass the time while waiting for our food.

Younger children improve their fine motor abilities while playing card games in addition to acquiring intellectual and logical concepts. Strength and dexterity will increase as they hold and handle the cards. The two hands will practice their bilateral coordination by shuffling the cards together.

Gameschooling is a fantastic way to support children in their weak areas as well as to strengthen bonds and boost self-esteem. Games come in a wide variety of styles and price ranges. There is a way to incorporate gameschooling into your homeschool, no matter what your objectives are.

Whether you use games, imaginative play, role-playing, or any other playful idea that comes to mind, remember how crucial play is to your children's growth and development. More, though, remember how incredible an opportunity we homeschoolers have when it comes to building strong relationships with our kids as well in cultivating amazing sibling relationships all in the name of fun!

Try This!

- **Play is pleasurable and spontaneous:** Surprise your child with an unexpected playdate, outing, or a new game. Let them choose activities that they find enjoyable and exciting.
- **Play reduces stress:** Create a calm and relaxing play environment. Incorporate soothing activities like drawing, storytelling, or building with blocks to help your child unwind.
- **Encourage free play:** Designate specific time for unstructured play where your child can decide what to do. Provide open-ended toys like building blocks, art supplies, or dress-up costumes.
- **Promote problem-solving:** Introduce puzzles, riddles, or board games that require your child to solve challenges and make decisions.
- **Foster emotional intelligence:** Engage in role-play scenarios with your child to help them understand and manage emotions. Use dolls or action figures to act out different feelings and resolutions.
- **Support autonomy:** Allow your child to make choices about their play activities. For example, let them decide whether they want to build a fort, paint a picture, or play a game.
- **Embrace creative play:** Encourage your child to engage in imaginative play by providing props and costumes for role-playing, or suggest they create their own stories with toys or drawings.
- **Promote social play:** Organize playdates with other children, board game nights, or team activities that encourage cooperation and communication.

- **Nurture play throughout life:** Continue to play games and engage in enjoyable activities with your child, even as they grow older. Show that play remains important in adulthood.
- **Gameschooling:** Use educational games or interactive apps to make learning enjoyable. For example, play math games together to reinforce math concepts or explore history through interactive apps.
- **Maintain a balance:** Set boundaries for screen time, work, and leisure. Establish a schedule that allows for both productive tasks and time for family play and relaxation.

6 | Six Key Learning Skills

Education is a social process. Education is growth. Education is not a preparation for life; education is life itself.

— John Dewey

There will be times when you walk into a room and no one there is quite like you . . . until the day you begin to share your stories. And all at once, in the room where no one else is quite like you, the world opens itself up a little wider to make some space for you."

— From *The Day You Begin* by Jacquelin Woodson

Andrew and his friends Emma and Brandon spent hours in the woods every day. They were lucky enough to live near each other, and all homeschooled, so they met at their special place in the woods every day once their parents had cut them loose from their school and chores. Sometimes one of the siblings would tag along, but mostly it was the three of them.

One bright day, with the sun dancing through the treetops, the three of them set off into the woods with excitement. They'd planned this for weeks, had sketches and supplies, and a packed lunch. The plan – to build a fort, constructed just for them. They roamed through the woods, searching for the perfect spot. Brandon, the visionary, was the first to spot it — a small clearing where the sun's rays gently peeked through.

The process of building their fort was a true collaboration. Branches were collected. Logs were dragged. And the twine they'd brought in with them was measured and cut. They arranged the logs and branches into walls leaned around a large tree. Emma was the creative force and decorated the entrance with a curtain of draped vines. Andrew used logs to create a small table and stools. Hour after hour, they pieced together the hideaway that would become their haven. They held club meetings there, played make believe, told tall tales, and enjoyed their friendship.

Dr. Kathy Hirsh-Pasek, co-author, along with Roberta Michnick Golinkoff, of *Becoming Brilliant: What Science Tells Us About Raising Successful Children*, tells us that there are six key skills that will help kids become thinkers and that they are crucial to helping them become "contributing members of their communities and good citizens as they forge a fulfilling personal life." These six key skills— the 6 Cs, as they are known—are collaboration, communication, content, critical thinking, creativity, and confidence. Furthermore, according to Dr. Patricia K. Kuhl, "When you look at the studies on very young human babies, even newborns, they are captivated by the human face." According to Kuhl, the fixation with the face has its roots in human evolution and can be explained by a complex neural network made to understand social cues, or what neuroscientists refer to as the *social brain*.

The Best Thing. . .

The best thing about homeschooling was being
super close to all of my siblings and parents.
—Drew, 19

The fort builders not only worked together, socially collaborating on a shared goal, they communicated, added in creativity, a bit of critical thinking, and likely boosted their collective confidence as well. Self-directed collaborative play like this fosters strength and resilience in our kids, taps into Hirsh-Pasek's 6 Cs, and makes learning social all at once. Incorporating social learning and the 6 Cs into our homeschooling helps kids be ready to forge careers in a future that will likely look nothing like what we parents have experienced. The education system is becoming more and more information-driven, so let's give our kids the edge by empowering them with these key skills and grow world changers!

Why Learn About the 6 Cs?

Playful learning centers around active, engaged, meaningful, socially interactive, iterative, and joyful activities. When we consider play-based learning, it prompts the question of what knowledge and skills are essential for thriving in today's world. We can help kids build the 6 Cs through our play-based, interest-led homeschool – especially since all of them are firmly grounded in the principles of learning and build on each other.

For instance, without the ability to collaborate effectively, kids may find it challenging to become proficient communicators since they have not yet grasped the nuances of sensitivity and appropriate responses in relationships. This integration of the 6 Cs parallels the process of reading, a practice also dependent on these very skills. While reading is often perceived as a singular skill within a specific content area, research shows that the process of learning to read draws on a child's communication abilities, including oral language and a rich vocabulary, as well as their critical thinking skills, as not everything in print is necessarily accurate.

While the 6 Cs build on one another, they aren't stuck in a rigid order. Kids can have the flexibility to follow diverse paths in developing their 6 Cs skills. Even the *C* of *content* doesn't need to be tied to a specific curriculum manual. Instead, the 6 Cs present a model that parents can, and should, adapt to align with the unique interests and backgrounds of their kiddos.

The 6 Cs interconnect over time and with experience, making them an integral part of a dynamic learning system. For example, a child may excel as a communicator, but need more refinement of their critical thinking abilities. Kids may also need help in transferring their 6 Cs skills across different contexts, like a child who is a great writer but struggles to communicate with teammates on the soccer field. This makes it even more important to recognize and develop each of the 6 Cs.

Collaboration

Years ago I taught a class at our homeschool co-op based off a kit I purchased from a science supply company. The kit was a rotting log microhabitat in a small, plastic aquarium. Inside were a variety of organisms like millipedes, pill bugs, Tenebrio beetles, Bess bugs, and crickets, along with moss, soil, log pieces, and leaf litter. The kids loved learning about the inhabitants of the microhabitat and doing the experiments I had planned for them. Well, *most* of the kids loved it. Molly, my daughter and ten at the time, was not a nature-lover. In fact, she despised creepy-crawly things, and concocted a plan to get out of completing any of the work we did that semester after I told her and several other squeamish kiddos during the first class they should at least try touching the insects, or at the very least, stick close to the table so they could hear what I was teaching.

She countered that she and her friends could learn as much about those organisms by reading or looking up websites about decomposers, specifically the inhabitants of a rotting log. After thinking about it, she proposed a deal. If I gave her and her friends the time in class to research the organisms and their habitat, they'd use that research to write, direct, and present a short play entitled, "Life in a Rotting Log," to the rest of the co-op at the end of the semester. I agreed, and they held up their end of the bargain, researching quietly in the corner, then convincing their co-op-mates to work on the play with them at lunch time. They cast the show, held rehearsals, came up with costume ideas their friends pulled together from things they had at home, and on the last day of the session, they performed the play they'd collaborated on.

Kids are always watching the adults around them. We can set powerful examples for them with the smallest of efforts, especially if we take time to think past our often immediate need to gain compliance to the actual outcome we're hoping to achieve. I could have told Molly that the class was supposed to focus on hands-on science and experiential learning, and that she needed to try to touch the bugs we were studying each week. Or, I could have sent her out in the hallway to work and kept everyone else inside, as her friends weren't as completely anti-bug as she was. In fact, each of them handled the organisms at one point or another, and one of those sweet playwrights had her mom order the same kit for their home so she could raise them herself.

The Best Thing. . .

I can pick and choose what I want to learn and how I want to learn it. This includes the books I want to read. I also get to see my brothers grow up.

—Brooklyn, 17

By changing up my expectations and hearing Molly out, I taught her that there is more than one way to demonstrate learning. I valued her ideas and input, and empowered her to go an alternate route toward mastery. Creating something collaboratively with friends, like writing and performing a play, can give kids opportunities to expand their thinking and grow their emotional intelligence.

Collaboration lies at the heart of human interaction, playing a pivotal role in both social and educational development. When we collaborate, we invite diverse perspectives into our lives. We work with people from different backgrounds, experiences, and worldviews. This diversity serves as a window into a broader understanding of the world, fostering inclusivity, acceptance, and open-mindedness. One of the most significant rewards of collaboration is the cultivation of critical thinking skills. In collaborative settings, individuals must analyze problems, brainstorm ideas, and make decisions collectively. This process encourages us to evaluate various options before reaching a consensus. The ability to think critically, a skill honed through collaboration, is an asset both in our social interactions and our educational journey.

Drama, ballet, and music classes are also excellent settings for collaborating since kids need to work together for performances. Service projects can teach kids the importance of working together on a bigger scale and show them their role in the community. To create environments that encourage collaboration, it's crucial to understand how children develop.

For example, the Great Lakes Science Center, one of our favorite places to go in the early years of our homeschooling, had a cool setup with a bucket hanging from a crane. The children in the play area would naturally gravitate to it, and instinctively collaborate. One kiddo would hold the lever down so the bucket stayed closed, while another posted as the sentry who watched to alert the lever-bearer when the bucket was full. The rest of the children pumped pit balls through the vacuum tunnel that swept them up into the bucket, cheering as it filled more and more. Once the bucket was full, the sentry alerted everyone, and the kids all dived into the center while the lever-bearer release the cargo, spilling balls onto the pile of kids in the pit. Even though the kids didn't know each other, they naturally teamed up to move the balls and fill the bucket, showing how collaboration can be part of an activity.

In college classes, collaboration is promoted by having group activities in the syllabus. Students must do group-based research presentations and are encouraged to study together for exams. This approach recognizes that learning is often more effective when done together, resulting in a better final product. This doesn't mean there's no downtime or independent work. It just emphasizes that we need to develop social skills alongside our independent ones, leading them into the adult world where they'll need to collaborate on teams in the workplace.

We often focus on learning facts and content, and assume that social skills will develop on their own. However, these soft skills also need practice, and there are many opportunities to help kids transition from being independent to working in teams. One thing I've learned as the homeschooling mom to a graduate-turned-entrepreneur is that while passion-driven learning and growing one's own business is often a solo journey, even the most creative and driven kids and young adults will need to know how to work with others – whether that is when taking on a freelance project, finding new clients, presenting oneself to a potential client, or finding other creative entrepreneurs to network with. There's no growth without collaboration.

Collaboration is crucial for many things we want for our kids. It's essential for happiness as it leads to friendships and self-control. Research has shown that people who have a sense of belonging and social connections are healthier and happier. Collaborative work also benefits cognitive skills because it balances out one person's weaknesses with another's strengths. That's why collaboration often leads to better outcomes than working alone. Being part of a community fuels our desire to make a positive impact on the world.

But the benefits of collaboration aren't just educational. They extend to our kids' social lives. In working together, kids develop interpersonal skills like empathy, teamwork, and leadership. These skills forge strong relationships and help kids thrive. Beyond the individual benefits, collaboration nurtures a sense of belonging and unity within a family, group, or community. As we collaborate, we learn adaptability. We must adjust to different working styles, personalities, and approaches. This adaptability, honed through collaboration, is a life skill that serves us well in a world where societies, technologies, and workplaces are in constant flux.

Collaboration isn't just a means to an end. It's a journey of personal and collective growth. It's the synergy of diverse minds working together, fostering understanding, tolerance, and progress. It's the heartbeat of society, a dance of individuals coming together to shape a brighter, more harmonious future — a future our kids will shape together.

Communication

Communication skills are the building blocks of collaboration. When we give our kids plenty of chances to interact with others, they naturally get better at expressing their ideas, actively listening to others, and giving constructive feedback. These skills aren't just for school; they come in handy in everyday life, making it easier for them to connect with others.

Speaking clearly so people understand you, writing in a way that gets your message across, and really listening to what others have to say are the skills of effective communicators. If we want our kids to be happy and successful in their relationships, they need to learn to talk to others respectfully. Name-calling? Nope, not acceptable. Sharing their feelings honestly? Absolutely. In a global world, these skills are essential. Whether it's collaborating, sharing information, or persuading others, good communication is key. It doesn't matter if it's in the fields of science, government, medicine, or even sports and entertainment.

Effective communicators are those who can put themselves in the other person's shoes. But not all kids (or even adults) are equally good at this. Take the online world, for example. Kids sometimes hide behind the anonymity of the internet to say things they'd never say in person. Tina recalls a time her daughter Olivia was playing Roblox, and another player started saying mean things in the chat. It made Olivia uncomfortable, so she called Tina over, and they reported the player together. They even had a great conversation during dinner about how some people enjoy being mean online because they can hide behind a screen. Olivia and Tina made a plan for dealing with such situations in the future.

Some people argue that kids need to be in school to develop their social skills and have meaningful conversations. But I'd argue they're wrong. Many schools these days focus more on stuffing kids with information rather than encouraging conversations. They still follow the old model of having students sit quietly and absorb information. But communication is a two-way street that requires understanding your audience.

The Best Thing. . .

We have the freedom to travel in our RV across the country. I love having new experiences with places and cultures. We've climbed mountains, visited "wonders" and historic places, swam in famous lakes and beaches, and have met amazing people with different accents along the way. Oh – and the food! Trying new foods in each region of our country is really cool.

—Tyler, 17

Only when we grasp this and help our kids learn naturally can we really broaden their horizons and engage their minds. For younger kids, pretend play works wonders; they can understand others better when they take on different roles in their games. Older kids can benefit from acting in theater productions, which helps them develop empathy and a better understanding of others. In today's digital age, online communication skills are just as crucial as face-to-face ones. As Jim Rohn, the author of *The Keys to Success*, said, "If you just communicate, you can get by. But if you skillfully communicate, you can work miracles."

Back when my kids were younger, we used to have weekly family meetings to create opportunities for conversation. We often discussed our differences, individual strengths and weaknesses, and the idea that our family was stronger because of the unique contributions each of us brought to the table. We wanted our kids to understand that sometimes they needed to be alone, and sometimes they needed the support of a family member. We used these meetings to teach open and honest communication through role-playing.

Now, when one of our kids needs some alone time or some help with something, they know they can tell the rest of us. I remember a time at the Great Lakes Science Center watching a movie in the iMax theater. My kids had grown up in that place as, with a ten-year age span between my oldest and the youngest, it was one of the few places where everyone could find something to enjoy. We were sitting in the theater: me plying then-two-year-old Isaac with snacks: six-year-old Logan staring raptly at the baby chipmunk on the screen; eight-year-old Molly sitting as sweet as can be; and twelve-year old Trevor slumped in his chair, pretending to be bored. The music changed, and I felt a hand clamp down on my arm. I looked over to see my Logan, eyes wide, face pale, terror screaming from her expression while her fingers dug deep enough to bruise. Immediately, I snatched Isaac up, grabbed my bag and Logan's arm with my free hand, and pushed our way out of the theater, whispering for Molly and Trevor to meet us at the tables (our meet-up place at the science center) when the movie ended.

As we made it into the hall and the door closed quietly behind me, I led the kids toward the tables, and told Logan, "You know, the chipmunk is going to make it." She nodded, still pale, and we found a table. While I pulled out my emergency stash of snacks, bottled water, and a tin of Spot It! cards, I reminded her again that the chipmunk was the star of the nature movie we'd just left, so it was going to make it to the end alive, and the owl that had appeared on screen along with the tension-implying music, wasn't going to be successful in its hunt.

Logan has anxiety, and while we usually know what is likely to trigger a panic attack, sometimes one comes on unexpectedly, but because we communicate regularly and share in each other's struggles and successes, every family member is there to support the others. Logan calmed down as we snacked and played, and the movie ended with Molly and Trevor bounding out to meet us and share that the chipmunk did, indeed, survive the hunt and its first year of life.

The Best Thing. . .

My favorite part of homeschooling is being at
home with the people I love.

—Jeni, 9

Communication truly sets the stage for what we want for our children. It's like a bridge to mastering subjects like reading, math, science, and the arts. They say that children first learn to read and then read to learn. Without strong language and communication skills, early reading lessons wouldn't get them far. After all, sounding out C-A-T doesn't mean much if they don't already know the word *cat*. Kids learn new words through conversations, the kind that's full of open-ended questions and dialogue.

Words, language, and stories are the foundation of communication. They're like the building blocks that let children share their thoughts and understand others. Our success as a society relies on our ability to communicate effectively. Both hard and soft skills are built on this foundation.

Content

Somehow our culture got duped into thinking that content is the only *C* of value—parents, schools, and the learning industry overvalue it. Education, even when it comes to homeschooling, has been distilled to what kids learn instead of *how* they learn it, making the soft skills – the thinking skills their futures depend on – almost an afterthought. It is time to ask how we can educate children in a way that promotes deep learning. We need to stretch the definition of *content* to include HOW to find the answers needed to solve the problem and HOW to put together the information and resources to make it possible. We ask two questions here: how do we learn content in the first place and what will it take to learn content in a deep way that allows us to use it in the world?

Homeschooling gives us a huge advantage over the traditional school models. We can teach our kids to value the process of learning as much as the outcome. In fact, I often tell parents when they ask, that one of my main goals in teaching my children at home is to help them know that nothing they want to learn is further than an asked question, Google search, video streamed, book read, or conversation with a mentor away. They can find out the answers to everything they're curious about, and so I want to empower them in the knowledge that they should never "know everything" because there's always more to know.

Yet, even when we homeschool, it's easy to fall back on the teaching of facts rather than teaching our children how to learn, how to evaluate information, and how to draw integrative and innovative conclusions. Dr. Frank Smith, author of *Insult to Intelligence: The Bureaucratic Invasion of Our Classrooms*, believes that one of the biggest issues in education is that students learn exactly what they're taught. When we limit learning only to content that changes daily, we doom our kiddos to becoming obsolete before they even graduate from high school. It's not that content is unimportant. Having a well of knowledge frees our minds to solve problems. Think about the multiplication tables. We automatically remember that $7 \times 4 = 28$ in what feels like a nanosecond. It's incredibly efficient. This skill lets our teens quickly compute how many of those $4.00 on-sale shirts they can buy to round out their closet.

Content is crucial.

But we must go beyond teaching what is known. If our children are to have learning agility, they must learn how to think creatively so that they can assemble old parts to serve new functions. They must have the mental flexibility to change course as they solve problems. And they must be in environments that present them with those problems so they can reuse what they know. This will not happen by using bubble tests that have only one right answer.

The Best Thing. . .

I get to do lots of projects!

—Joanna, 12

I'm not completely against testing. If a test assesses actual learning, is used to inform the teaching, or to figure out where a child needs more support, then it's a wonderful *tool*. But when testing becomes the focus, we're lost. I remember being the student in my history classes who would cram for tests and learn content just in time, then forget it soon after the test results came back. I didn't learn much history. I retained it in my short-term memory to check off a few boxes.

I recalled earlier in this book the conversation I had with one of my children after they finished a phone call with a friend who was writing a history paper. After our conversation, and that kiddo's deep dive into books, videos, and other resources to learn what their friend was learning, they showed me a sketchbook filled with colorful notes they'd taken of their research.

A year later, that kiddo can still tell me all about that time period and what impact it's had on our current world.

Content is learned best when it's meaningful, and when we focus on testing, it becomes meaningless. Kids take tests in isolation, without the benefits of collaboration, communication, or even critical and creative thinking. They're regurgitating facts and figures. Homeschooling allows us to craft environments that support happy, healthy, thinking, caring, and social children who become collaborative, creative, competent, and responsible citizens tomorrow. And content by itself is never enough.

It's hard to break free from this mentality, especially because the first question most people ask (if it's not the "socialization" question) is "what curriculum do you use?" Remember, though, your kiddos' educations aren't limited to what a curriculum says it should be; it's a part of everyday life. You have so many opportunities to inspire your children's curiosity, and it's all about making learning fun, engaging, and relevant. And you can do this with whatever curriculum you use, or without a curriculum altogether!

Children are learning all the time. Whether you're at the pharmacy, the supermarket, or on a family trip, there are teachable moments waiting to be seized. Encourage your kids to ask questions and explore their world. When children are having fun learning in their everyday life, it often spills over into their formal education, making them more excited about learning in general. They often don't even realize how much they are learning.

Roger and Emily are coaching clients whose kiddo Jeremy had just entered his junior year when they sought support. Jeremy didn't like to do busy work, struggled to stay focused, and wanted more autonomy in his learning, but at the same time, spent much of his day avoiding his work and playing video games. His parents had followed a very eclectic style of home-schooling, using very little curriculum aside from math, and letting Jeremy learn through podcasts, videos, reading, and conversations. They had pulled him out of school to homeschool in first grade because he was bright, underachieving, and spent much of the time he was bored disrupting the kids around him. They'd been working with him through various therapies and help for the past several years, and were hoping the four of us could work together on an educational plan.

He'd been seeing a child psychologist and had a great relationship with her, so when he confessed to her that he didn't think he was actually learning anything anyway, so there was no point in spending his time on anything other than video games as he wasn't going to be able to get into a good school anyway, she suggested he try taking a standardized achievement test for his age and see if that was true so they could make a plan for how to handle the rest of his high school years. He and his parents agreed.

The Best Thing. . .

I like having my mom's undivided attention.

—Brandon, 12

Jeremy tested beyond the high school levels that capped the test in most areas. In the few he scored at- or below-grade level, the missing information was simply related to a content gap because the topic hadn't sparked an interest yet. When we talked, the four of us discussed Jeremy's hope for his future, and what he wanted to study in college. Then we made a plan to fill in the gaps he wanted to fill from his test results and take classes or do projects related to the areas he knew would give him a leg up when it came time for college applications. He had a new focus, and realized that, despite his educational experience not looking like his public school friends' did, he was not only learning, but actually ahead of his grade level. He also had a renewed trust for his parents' instincts about his homeschooling.

It's not unusual for kids who are homeschooled using nontraditional methods to think they're missing out or that they're not learning when they see what kids in school are doing. But, when we show them how much they know, empower them to find solutions and information, and build up their confidence, they'll shine.

And don't forget the power you have as a homeschooling parent to motivate by example. Your kids are watching you. If you're excited about learning, your children will be too. Everyone has areas of expertise, so give yourself credit for what you know. But also be open to learning new things. It's okay not to be an expert in everything, and showing your children you're willing to explore new information sets a fantastic example. Plus, it's a great way to bond with your kids. So, whether it's baking, speaking a foreign language, or any other skill you possess, share it with your children and let them learn from your experiences.

Remember, too, learning doesn't only happen at home. There's a world of opportunities out there waiting to be explored. Museums, parks, and community events can all be fantastic resources for learning. Take, for example, visiting a colonial site when your child is studying the Pilgrims or exploring a farm when they're learning about where food comes from. Local universities and colleges often have museums or exhibits that cater to kids' interests. These trips can be educational and incredibly fun for the whole family.

Tap into your child's personal interests. If they're fascinated by a topic, dive into it *with* them. Visit the library and let them choose books that excite them. Reading together can be a wonderful bonding experience. Encourage them to explore the arts, be it through theater camps, art classes, or attending local performances. These experiences not only nurture their creative side, but also help develop valuable skills.

The road to true learning is paved with experiences you share with your children. You don't have to overthink the content, dump information on your kids, or break the bank to create a stimulating learning environment. Grab those teachable moments as they happen and show your kiddos that education is an exciting lifelong journey.

Critical Thinking

Throughout that journey, you get a front-row seat to watching learning and understanding unfold, and to helping your kids make sense of their world. Critical thinking plays a crucial role as our kids discover who they're meant to be. It's like the secret ingredient that helps them navigate their complex world and make informed choices. You want your kids to thrive, so it's important to encourage them to question, analyze, and think for themselves.

With the internet bombarding all of us with information, it's easy to get swept away by flashy promises or others' opinions. Remember those programs that promised they'd teach your baby to read in just a few days? Or others that swore your kiddo would grow to be a genius if you just played the tape for hours each afternoon? We all want the best for our kids, but let's face it, attending a specific preschool or following a "guaranteed genius" program online won't guarantee them a job at Google. In today's information age, it's not about how much you know, but how well you can connect the dots and think outside the box. That's where critical thinking comes in.

The Best Thing. . .

I love that I can learn as fast as my brain wants to.
—Ambrose, 6

When Trevor was tiny, Baby Einstein videos were all the rage. We'd watch each afternoon and I'd pore over books and magazines searching for the tip that would make me the parent I dreamed of being. He was smart, no question about it, but it had less to do with me showing him videos or reading to him while he was in the womb than it did with his nature, brain, and curiosity. If I did anything right during that time, it was to encourage his explorations, ask questions, and encourage him to share his observations. Listening more than I talk has been my parenting secret weapon for more than twenty years now. I want my kids to think for themselves, puzzle things out, draw their own conclusions, and then talk (or debate) with me about them.

You can teach critical thinking by modeling and asking tough questions. For example, when Trevor was taking a writing class at the local community college, and was evaluating others' writing as an exercise at home, he couldn't just say that a portion of the author's research was poorly done. He needed to explain why. Being critical of one's own thoughts and arguments is the first step in thinking critically. Knowing how to craft a good argument is something all kids need to learn. We can all improve our critical thinking skills.

Asking why, reading aloud, playing games, and sharing funny tales are effective ways to encourage your child's critical thinking abilities. Games encourage critical thinking because they teach kids about rules and how to spot them when they are broken. However, they must first learn the rules. We have all seen our kiddos argue with one another about who goes first, why that move didn't count, and all sorts of other things. However, disagreeing is good and encourages the growth of critical thinking. We can observe our children settle these issues with their siblings and peers if we teach them how to disagree with others, but do so in a respectful manner. Communication includes negotiation skills, and teaching kids to be critical thinkers is a crucial life skill.

Storytelling is a lost art, and a good storyteller is not only entertaining, but also filled with lifelong lessons. You can share your experiences with your kids. My kids love hearing about what I did when I was younger. And they never stop asking questions. To gain knowledge about the world and cultivate a critical mindset, one must ask questions.

Reading books is another fantastic way to encourage critical thinking. When the story takes an unexpected turn, your child will start asking questions and imagining alternative endings. This sparks their creativity and their ability to question why things are the way they are.

Kids often question us about why people behaved the way they do. *Why did Addy say those things about Erin, Mom? I thought they were friends.* Children are highly motivated to understand what makes others behave a certain way because if they can understand why other people behave in unexpected ways, it reduces some of the unpredictability in their social relationships. Instead of dismissing their questions, we can ask what they think or how they feel about the situation. We can ask what they would have done in Addy's position or in Erin's. These are conversations and prompts that encourage kids' critical thinking and help them solve puzzles. They need to realize that not everyone who dislikes someone calls them names or takes advantage of them; they do not have to simply accept the way things are. Children need to be encouraged to think critically and consider other possibilities.

Critical thinking opportunities are everywhere you go with your children. From art class to theater rehearsals and everyday conversations, you can encourage them to ask questions, explore why things are the way they are, and develop that all-important critical perspective.

To create an environment that fosters critical thinking, it all starts with respect. Show your children that their questions and ideas matter. Even from a young age, they should feel that their curiosity is valued. And remember, respectful parenting not only nurtures their minds, but also strengthens your bond with them. As parents, we're guiding the next generation of inventors, entrepreneurs, scientists, and engineers. They're the visionaries and futurists who see opportunities and solutions where others don't. Critical thinking is the pathway to success, and it's something you can nurture in your children every day. Keep those questions coming, encourage them to think differently, and let them know that they can shape the world with their innovative ideas.

The Best Thing. . .

I love not having to go to a regular school. It's cool to stay home, learn, and have fun all at the same time.

—Mae, 11

Creativity

Critical thinking is essential, but it's like the first step of a beautiful journey. The next stop is creative innovation. To truly succeed, our children need to know how to take all that knowledge and information and create something entirely new from it. It's about thinking differently and solving problems in unique ways.

Creativity isn't the same as intelligence. It's about thinking outside the box, coming up with new solutions from old parts – like being a master tinkerer. Sir Ken Robinson, author of *Out of Our Minds: Learning to Be Creative*, says many people believe that creativity is just for those special people, the artistic geniuses. But that's not the case at all. Creativity is within reach for all of us. He also asserts the misconception that creativity is all about special activities, like the arts, is bogus. While the arts do thrive on creativity, Robinson's point is that creativity plays a role in everything we do, not just painting or dancing. It's in everyday innovations, like the printing press, which brought this book into your hands, or in the ideas we share. Creativity is everywhere, not just in the arts.

Robinson says, too, when we think of creativity, we often imagine someone eccentric or wild, like a person running in circles with a jester's hat. Most creative folks are pretty much like you and me. They don't have to have crazy hair like Albert Einstein or wear outrageous outfits like Madonna. In fact, they look just like everyday people. It's because creativity is a combination of education, skill, imagination, and discipline. It's not about your appearance but what's going on in your mind.

He contends that creativity can be taught. And here's the best part – it's about breaking free from what psychologists call *functional fixedness*. This is a fancy way of saying we need to break out of the habit of thinking that a stapler is only for connecting pages together. It can also be a doorstop, a paperweight, or whatever you can imagine. Creativity is all about thinking beyond the obvious and being open to new ideas.

So, how can you nurture creativity in your kids and help them become the inventors, entrepreneurs, and big thinkers of tomorrow? Encourage them to explore, ask questions, and challenge the norm. Let them draw outside the lines and think beyond the stapler and staples.

The Best Thing. . .

We can take lots of cool classes and we can take
any day off that we want and do whatever like go
to fun hotels and stuff.

—Lincoln, 12

My sixteen-year-old Molly once sang the song *Audition* from the movie *La La Land*, and this excerpt from the lyrics have stuck:

A bit of madness is key
To give us new colors to see
Who knows where it will lead us?
And that's why they need us
So bring on the rebels
The ripples from pebbles
The painters, and poets, and plays
And here's to the fools who dream
Crazy as they may seem

In the book *What Do You Do with an Idea?* by Kobi Yamada, a child has a fantastic idea, and it's not just any idea – it's a "brilliant" one. The character takes us on a journey of grit and determination as they bring their idea to life, facing challenges and growing more confident throughout the story. Creativity is all around us, waiting to take flight. It's in our shadows, in the trees, and in our vibrant imaginations. Like the song lyrics suggest, it takes a little madness, experimentation, rebellion, and we're not sure where it'll take us, but creativity pays off.

Often, we don't give creativity the space it deserves or explore it fully. We've seen a decline in creativity, as Robinson points out, but we can make sure to infuse our own homeschools with it. Ask if you allow yourself to be creative in your daily life. Being creative means taking risks and trying things that might not always turn out as expected. You can start small, like whipping up a new recipe for dinner with spices you've never used before. Sure, it might not be a culinary masterpiece, but your kids will remember your effort. My friend Pam tells the story of the time she realized belatedly that it was Dr. Suess's birthday, and on a whim, dyed the scrambled eggs green and served green eggs and ham for breakfast. Little dashes of creativity go a long way. Her kids are now teens, with one graduated, and they still remember that breakfast.

When was the last time you tried your hand at art? You don't have to be Picasso. The key is to give it a go, even if your attempt at drawing an apple ends up looking more like squiggles. We're often held back by the fear of not being good enough, but the truth is, creativity knows no boundaries. It can be fun for your kids to have you sit with them and try their lessons out too. I recently signed up Logan for a seven-day cartooning challenge. Seven unique lessons in seven days meant we were both covering reams of paper with marker and pencil, drawing popular video game characters using techniques neither of us had tried before. By the end of the week, the other kids – even the twenty-one-year-old – had joined in and we'd signed up for the membership the cartoonist offered at the end of the trial week. We now have hundreds of on-demand cartooning lessons at our fingertips, and we're all enjoying the creativity. (Though my kids are definitely better at cartooning than I am.)

The Best Thing. . .

> Rainy days are great for reading my favorite books. I can curl up in my blanket and take my time. My family and I also enjoy cooking and working on projects together.
>
> —Quinn, 11

How about dedicating just fifteen to twenty minutes a day to letting your kids unleash their inventiveness? They can take that old, broken vacuum cleaner or the box from your new dishwasher and turn it into something magical. Encourage them to build forts from sofa cushions or create family portraits, even if they're still mastering the art of drawing. We belonged to a co-op years ago that offered clubs during the afternoons, and I facilitated a maker's club where I provided recyclables, craft supplies, glue guns, and whatever else we could find or collect, and I'd give the kids a theme and thirty minutes to create. At the end of that time, they'd clean up, and then take turns presenting their take on the theme using the materials at hand. The creative things the kids came up with inspired me.

There are so many ways to encourage creativity in your everyday. When you travel, your kids can keep journals filled with mementos and their stories. Your backyard can be an incredible place for creativity to blossom. Bark from trees can become art, leaves can be placed in collages, and water can serve as paint as you experiment with the art form. Your kids can discover the magic of shadows and create vibrant sidewalk chalk masterpieces. Inside your home, pots and pans turn into drums, bottles become wind instruments, and the entire house becomes an orchestra. You can put on shows based on your favorite stories. Outside your home, look for opportunities to use everyday tools in new ways or to reshape activities and routines. It's all about encouraging fresh perspectives and imaginative thinking.

You can inspire creativity by visiting museums, library exhibits, and community art displays. When your children see that real people express themselves visually, they'll be more inclined to try it themselves. Music and drama are abundant too, from community performances to professional events. Get involved, even if it's a game of charades – your children will follow suit.

Creative thinkers are the ones who will have a future filled with possibilities. But here's the thing – creativity often follows unique paths. This is why we need to equip our children with not only knowledge, but also the confidence and persistence to move forward, even when faced with potential setbacks. Creative thinkers are explorers, pattern finders, path creators, and entrepreneurs, and they rarely take *no* for an answer.

When we cultivate an environment of creative collaboration, authentic exploration, and critical questioning, our kids become independent thinkers. They'll shape their own futures and do it with confidence.

Confidence

Confidence has two key parts. The first is all about the willingness to give things a try. As Wayne Gretzky famously said, "You miss 100% of the shots you don't take." Without confidence, it's tough for our kids to embrace new challenges and venture out of their comfort zones.

The second part is about persistence, or *grit* as coined by Angela Duckworth, author of *Grit: The Power of Passion and Perseverance*. It's about sticking with those long-term goals. Grit allows budding inventors to keep refining their ideas, continually experimenting until they get it just right. It helps kids dive headfirst into complex topics, even when they're initially puzzled. The difference between those who succeed and those who don't can often come down to confidence.

The Best Thing. . .

I get lots of love!

—Alex, 6

High-stakes tests and the relentless focus on grades is the exact opposite of what our kids need. Children need room to struggle; they shouldn't feel like they must understand everything instantly. Learning takes time, and we should reward each step in the process, especially when our young learners face inevitable failures along the way. This is one of the greatest advantages to homeschooling – parents can give their children room to struggle in a safe space, while being there to pick them up and encourage them without the high stakes of tests and grades. Teresa's daughter Eva took two years to master fourth-grade math. Teresa takes a mastery-based philosophy when it comes to the subjects she teaches her kids. In her opinion, there's no point in moving them on to the next level until they know the current content inside and out, particularly for a skill-based subject like math that builds from concept to concept. Once Eva mastered the concepts and consistently scored 95% or above on any assignment in the math book, Teresa moved her on to fifth-grade math. Her confidence was so high from getting the time she needed to succeed, that she completed the fifth-grade math program in less than half the year and is well on her way to completing sixth-grade math and being back on grade level.

Carol Dweck, author of *Mindset: Changing the Way You Think To Fulfill Your Potential*, believes that if we help kids see the brain as a muscle that gets stronger with exercise, they're more likely to persevere when they encounter roadblocks. Confidence is a game-changer when it comes to performance. Expectations play a huge role in achievement. If children are placed in situations where they're expected to fail, their performance nosedives. Their minds practically switch off, confirming those low expectations. But, put them in a situation where they're expected to shine, and they'll rise to the occasion.

Are you the kind of person who just barrels on, even when there are warning signs you should heed? Or maybe you tend to hesitate, wondering about where you stand and get stuck. Perhaps you're the type who thoroughly evaluates all angles and then takes a calculated risk after analyzing all the data. Or you may be the dare-to-fail visionary who questions the very foundations of a project or situation? As you consider this, think about the example you're setting for your kiddos. Those who barrel on tend to raise children who do the same. And those who give up in the face of difficulty can pave the way for children who don't learn to persevere.

Every child is unique; some are born confident, while others have to develop it over time. Remember your own childhood – were you the tree climber or the one who hesitated? Kids move at their own pace, but we all want them to have the confidence to make friends and tackle tough problems. You can help boost their confidence. For example, when it comes to social situations, some kids might feel like melting into the background when meeting new people. Others confidently make eye contact and offer a handshake. You can teach your kiddos this practice, and it can become a part of their routine when meeting new people. When Trevor was nineteen, he decided he wasn't getting out of the house enough as his freelance work kept him chained to the computer in his bedroom at home. He applied for a job at the local Chick-fil-A where several friends worked, figuring he could get out, score some free food on his shifts, earn some fun money, and see his friends each day. A win all around. After the interview, the manager commented on how articulate and put together he was. She said he was the first person she'd ever interviewed who looked her in the eye, shook her hand, and didn't take out his phone while they talked. He was stunned, figuring that these behaviors were simply common sense and the bare minimum expected at an interview.

Praising effort is a great way to build confidence in your kids. Instead of complimenting them for being smart, focus on their effort. This encourages them to take on new challenges and keep trying, even if they stumble along the way. When they do make mistakes, approach it with a neutral tone and ask them what happened. This engages them in deep thinking and helps them avoid repeating the same mistake next time.

When your kiddo needs a confidence boost, use their interests and provide more opportunities they'll love. If they enjoy ice-skating, take them more often or consider the occasional lesson. Help your kids develop competence to build their confidence in various aspects of their life. Remind them of the time and effort it took for them to become good at ice-skating, for example, as proof of their progress.

Confidence growth begins at home. It's the passport to daring big, persevering through challenges, and building your children's belief in themselves. It's a journey that begins when they're young, but extends throughout their lives, making our kids resilient, fearless, and confident for a lifetime.

Try This!

- **Empowering choice:** When your child expresses a reluctance to engage with certain activities, allow them to propose alternatives that align with their interests and comfort levels.
- **Family meetings:** Create opportunities for open communication within your family by holding regular family meetings.
- **Real-life conversations:** Encourage your child to engage in real-life conversations with you. Prompt your child to ask questions and explore their surroundings.
- **Teachable moments:** When visiting places like a historical site or farm, engage your child in discussions related to what they're learning or observing.
- **Passion-driven learning:** If your kids show a strong interest in a specific topic, support them in researching, exploring, and learning more about it.
- **Learning by example:** Serve as a role model for your child by demonstrating your own enthusiasm for learning. Let them see you explore new information and experiences.

- **Model critical thinking:** When discussing a news article or a book, ask open-ended questions like "Why do you think that happened?" or "What other perspectives can we consider?"

- **Use storytelling for critical thinking:** Share personal stories with your child, highlighting how you solved problems or made decisions.

- **Encourage disagreements:** Teach your child to disagree respectfully. When they have a disagreement with a sibling or friend, encourage them to express their viewpoint calmly and listen to the other side.

- **Reading aloud:** Read books with your child and pause to ask them questions about the story. Discuss the characters' motivations, choices, and possible alternative endings.

- **Creative innovation – Explore unconventional ideas:** Encourage your child to explore unconventional ideas and solutions. Provide materials for them to create something entirely new, like repurposing old household items for a creative project.

- **Embrace imperfection:** Show your child that making mistakes and not getting things perfect the first time are part of the learning process. Share examples of your own failures and what you learned from them.

- **Confidence – Effort over innate ability:** Praise your child's effort rather than just their innate ability. If they work hard on a school project, acknowledge their dedication and perseverance.

- **Teach persistence:** Teach your child the value of persistence. If they encounter challenges, encourage them to keep trying and provide support as they work through difficulties.

7 | Can Creativity Be Taught?

To live a creative life, we must lose our fear of being wrong.
—Joseph Chilton Pearce

People laugh at me because I use big words. But if you have big ideas, you have to use big words to express them, haven't you?"
—From *Anne of Green Gables* by Lucy Maud Montgomery

I was speaking at a homeschooling convention a few summers ago. It was a new convention location to me; I had never been to that particular state to speak before and was looking forward to meeting new people. More exciting for me was that a family from The Learner's Lab, the online community I host for families homeschooling out-of-the-box learners, was going to be there and I'd get to meet them. In the community, I teach master classes and host Q&As for parents, and I also teach live creative-thinking and social-emotional skills classes for the kids, so I'd "known" this family well online for a while, and I couldn't wait to see them in person.

When I'm at a speaking event, I'm all in. Those who have sat in on a session know I use the whole time I'm given, strive to share loads of practical takeaways, and stick around afterward to answer all questions attendees have. At this particular event, I walked into the first room I was speaking in and was greeted by this incredible family! I gave hugs, and promised to talk to the family members afterward, then headed up to the stage while they settled into their seats.

Once I was done with my session, I talked to dozens of moms, dads, and kids while this family waited. The two girls sat patiently, and the boy sketched. Finally, after what seemed to them like hours, I finished talking to the last mama about her anxious kiddo, and I was able to turn my attention to my "member" family. We chatted; the kids shared some of the projects they were working on, as well as some of the ideas they had for how I could improve the membership, and we made our way to the exhibit hall where Trevor was running the booth. The kids loved Trevor. He showed them card tricks and they chatted him up.

The Best Thing. . .

I like how you don't have to stop what you're doing to move on to the next subject when you're reading something you like. If I want to, I can work on one thing all day.

—Blake, 14

The next day, this family was waiting for me in my booth when my son Trevor and I arrived. They all had gifts for me – stories they'd written, pictures they drew, and from the boy who sat sketching, a comic strip depicting their meeting with me the day before, complete with a clock showing the long wait passing by, snippets of encouragement I'd given to other parents in speech bubbles, and Trevor's model-perfect swoopy hair. It was amazing.

Creativity can be innate in some, like this sweet boy. In others, it can be drawn out and cultivated. In all, it can – and should – be fostered and grown.

According to Sir Ken Robinson, "Creativity is as important as literacy." He believed that the best evidence of human creativity is one's trajectory through life. We design the life we lead. And this creativity, which appears in all the ways that people behave, is the heart of what it means to be a person. Most creative thinking is generated through collaboration and inspired by others' ideas. None of us exist alone. Even those who create alone draw inspiration from the past, from the ideas and accomplishments of other people.

The sweet gift of a comic strip drawn to depict the previous day sparked a conversation about drawing, art, and animation. He and I sat down to look through the animations he'd created on his iPad, with him showing me how he'd drawn inspiration from others whose work he'd studied. Creativity thrives in the art of collaboration. Throughout history, the greatest scientific, artistic, medical, and technological breakthroughs have come about from passionate collaboration among people with shared interests but different ways of thinking. It's a skill that we should nurture – the art of working together and embracing diversity instead of seeking uniformity.

The good news is that creativity can be taught. The common misconception is that it can't be taught because people don't fully understand it. We can teach fundamental creative thinking skills, much like we teach reading and math. These skills encourage different problem-solving approaches, emphasizing divergent thinking and creativity through analogies, metaphors, and visual thinking.

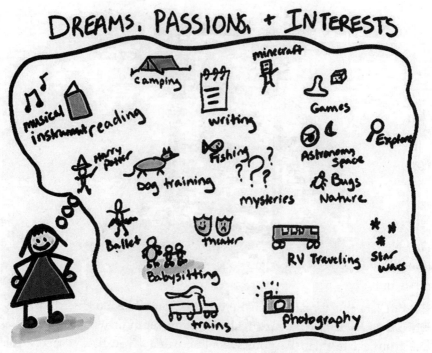

Colleen Kessler @ The Learner's Lab

A few years ago, I took a class about using visual facilitation to communicate ideas. I love this strategy for tackling abstract concepts like creativity and social-emotional learning, and often use strategies drawn from my learning when I teach in my membership community. For example, when I taught a class about having dreams and setting goals, I had the kids get creative by drawing pictures of a goal ladder after brainstorming some of their dreams, interests, and passions. They labeled them with their goals, and we talked about breaking down dreams and goals into manageable steps, or rungs on their dream ladders. When kids think visually, it sparks a different kind of energy. Breaking them out of their usual thoughts or strategies changes the dynamic, allowing creative thinking to flow. This is just one way to teach them specific skills that free up their creative thinking, emphasizing the value of diverse opinions.

But let's not forget personal creativity. Some kids do their best work when they connect with a particular medium, set of materials, or processes that truly excite them. As homeschooling parents, you have a special role in helping your children discover and nurture their own unique forms of creativity. It's a journey of exploration, learning, and growth, and you're the guiding force. So, keep fostering that creative spirit, and watch your children flourish in the world of imagination and innovation.

Elements of Creativity

Dr. E. Paul Torrance – researcher most well known for his Torrance Tests of Creative Thinking (TTCT), Thinking Creatively in Action and Movement (TCAM), Sounds and Images, Styles of Learning and Thinking, and the Creative Motivation Scale – believed that being creative requires bravery. Humans are creative learners by nature, and there are countless ways in which we can encourage our kids to be more creative. Perhaps the most crucial things we can do are to inspire them, support them, help them fall in love with something, and recognize then reward their progress. These elements are essential, and there are many ways to make them happen. Studies have shown that experiences in any visual art form, creative drama, media and reading programs, as well as certain instructional techniques or strategies, all help people be more creative. Simply put, giving kids opportunities to be open-ended and imaginative leads to more creative kids.

In its first year, members of The Learners Lab could complete activities related to the month's theme, then fill out a form to receive a badge in the mail to collect. As I'd just opened the community, I was doing all the work myself, and had designed the badges using clipart and fonts I owned. One of the sweetest kiddos ever, Nora, reached out to me through her mom's email and asked if I'd consider letting kids design the badges and use their artwork. As one of the driving motivations behind the community is to empower kids to think creatively, I agreed. She helped me create a submission form and guidelines, and we opened it up to members. Thirty kids have submitted badge designs so far, and I use every one of them. Nora showed bravery in sharing her creativity with me and others, and I'll always be grateful she had the courage to share such a fun idea.

Creativity is either helped or hampered by personality. Characteristics like being willing to take risks, being curious and searching, being independent in thought, being persistent and perseverant, being brave, being independent in judgment, being self-starting and showing initiative, having a sense of humor, and attempting difficult things all help facilitate creative thinking. Anything we do to promote these characteristics will inspire our kiddos to be more imaginative. Traits like arrogance and self-satisfaction, domineering and controlling behavior, negativism and resistance, fearfulness and apprehension, fault-finding and disagreeing, criticism of others, conformity, submissiveness to authority, and timidity all hinder creativity.

The Best Thing. . .

I love being able to go places in the middle of the day and the week without worrying about schoolwork because I have the flexibility to do it at any time not just during typical school hours.

—Keira, 13

Torrance built a framework that provides a suggested approach to fostering creativity. Homeschool parents can use its principles to help their children thrive. The Torrance framework for creative thinking emphasizes the development of creative thinking and problem-solving skills. It consists of four main components:

Fluency: This idea of creativity focuses on generating many ideas or solutions to a problem. Encourage your children to think beyond the obvious, fostering an environment where they feel free to express their ideas without judgment. You can use key words like *compare, identify, label, list, match, name, outline, paraphrase, predict, summarize, convert, count, define, explain,* or *describe.* Ask them to draw a picture and label the parts, list out twenty things that are blue, tell you how many additional uses they can find for a paperclip, or share all the facts they can think of about something they love.

Flexibility: Thinking flexibly involves the ability to approach a problem or task from different angles. Encourage your children to explore various perspectives and solutions, reinforcing the idea that there is often more than one way to solve a problem. You can use key words like *reason, incorporate, employ, assume, interpret, predict, integrate, encompass, absorb, include, engage, infer, deduce, decode,* and *unravel.* Ask them *what would happen if . . .?, how would a . . .?, how is ___ like ___?, how would you feel if . . .?,* or *how would you group . . .?*

Originality: Thinking with originality refers to the uniqueness of a solution or idea. Homeschool parents can foster originality by allowing their children to think outside the box, embrace their individuality, and not fear making mistakes. Original ideas often arise from a willingness to take risks. You can use key words like *compose, design, produce, create, integrate, change, rearrange, rebuild, reorganize,* and *rewrite.* Ask your kids to find inventive uses for everyday objects, what a unique way of folding sheets could be, to design a new type of car, or write a new and unusual title for a beloved book.

Elaboration: Elaboration means expanding on an idea by adding detail, depth, or complexity. Homeschool parents can nurture this aspect by encouraging their children to delve deeper into their interests and projects, helping them refine and develop their creative ideas. You can use key words like *assess, criticize, ascertain, consider, grade, judge, measure, pick,* and *test.* Ask your kids to tell you about the last book they read using as many details as possible, to describe all the characteristics of a favorite toy, or what they'd choose to add to something to make it better.

> ### The Best Thing. . .
>
> I don't have to sit at a desk for six hours. We just finish everything faster. Also, my mom is the best teacher!
>
> —Logan, 13

The Torrance framework of creative thinking provides homeschool parents with a valuable roadmap to nurture creativity in their children. By focusing on fluency, flexibility, originality, and elaboration, you can help your children develop the creativity they need to thrive in a rapidly changing world. By incorporating these principles into your homeschooling approach, you can unlock your children's creative potential and empower them to become innovative thinkers and problem-solvers.

The Power of Questions

One of the greatest things we can do to help cultivate creative and critical thinking in our kiddos is to teach them to question. Teaching your child how to explore and find answers to simple questions stimulates their young minds. You'll be surprised at how this simple act can spark more curiosity in them. Soon, they'll be asking you questions about everything that piques their interest.

As parents, we play a vital role in providing opportunities for our children to think critically and creatively from an early age. This is the foundation for success in their education, social experiences, and the challenges of adulthood. So, why are open-ended questions such a big deal? They're thought-provoking, engaging, and they allow your child to express their authentic selves. Homeschool parents can build the habit of questioning their kiddos and others around them, modeling how to be a thinker. Questioning and being questioned helps kids build essential reasoning skills and imagination – two key elements in shaping well-rounded individuals.

Open-ended questions are those that don't have a straightforward answer; they require more than a quick response. These questions ignite the flames of self-expression and independent thinking in your child. They're your secret weapon to stimulate critical thinking and foster their imagination. By asking open-ended questions, you'll help your child's curiosity and critical thinking skills flourish. They'll learn to explore, research, and discover information about themselves and the world around them.

And as they grow, they'll find answers about how things work, what they can do, and the resources available to them. It's a pathway for them to express themselves through writing and drawing, letting their creativity shine.

On the flip side, closed-ended questions are the ones that only get one- or two-word answers. They don't encourage your child to think beyond the obvious and don't promote the development of better questions. These are often called *observation* or *fact-based* questions. (Later in this chapter, I offer an extensive list of alternative open-ended questions.)

Examples of closed-ended questions include:

Did you have fun on your field trip?
Are you excited about your new baby sister?
What is your favorite book?
Do you have any pets?

The good news is there are plenty of opportunities to turn closed-ended questions into open-ended ones. I was speaking at a conference once about building resilience and confidence in kids after the release of my book, *Raising Resilient Sons: A Boy Mom's Guide to Building a Strong, Confident, and Emotionally Intelligent Family*, when a young mom came up to me afterward. I'd been talking about building strong family connections, and she told me she didn't think it was possible at this point and that she'd failed as a mom. Her tween only answered questions in single syllables. She didn't want to talk about her thoughts, interests, or feelings. She didn't engage with the family, so becoming more connected felt unattainable. Her daughter wasn't going to answer any question, let alone an open-ended one that took time and thought to answer.

The first thing I told her, and will reiterate for any homeschool parent reading this and feeling the same way, is that it's never too late. Novelist Jonathan Raymond says, "You can't know what you don't know. You can't know about things you have yet to discover." And it's true. If we spend time beating ourselves up for the things we messed up, and not looking toward using the new ideas, thoughts, and strategies we've discovered, how can we empower our children to learn from their mistakes? How can we teach them to question, innovate, and grow? We are our children's only intimate example of what parenting is, so we need to show them that we're still learning too. I told her to make little changes. Instead of asking if she had fun on the field trip, ask what her favorite part was and why. Instead of telling her that her painting was nice, ask her how she knew which colors to mix to achieve the smoky blue of the sky.

The Best Thing. . .

I get help one-on-one. I don't have to hurry to learn things.

—Finley, 10

When you're talking to your kids, you're not looking for them to simply answer the questions; you want them to share their story. Stories matter. Details matter. Open-ended questions are artful, probing, and meaningful. They tell your kids you care what they really think and want to know what's deeper. That you want to know them; really know them deeply. You want to give your kids a chance to come up with their own conclusions and consider things they might not have thought about before. When you spend time on the simple thoughts, ideas, and conversations when they're young, asking for more detail, and showing you care to know it all, they'll come to you with the bigger things later on. I promise.

As you sit down with your child, sharing conversations filled with open-ended questions, you're doing more than just exchanging words. You're encouraging a relationship that benefits you both for a lifetime. They learn that there's more than one way to see a situation, more than one answer to a question. Suddenly, the world becomes a place of endless possibilities, where learning never ceases, and understanding keeps evolving. With open-ended questions, they're not confined to a narrow path of predetermined answers. Their imagination is opened, allowing them to think beyond the ordinary. They trust themselves to think outside the box.

These questions are like a mental workout for your child's brain. As they grapple with the complexities of open-ended explorations, their cognitive abilities are stretched and strengthened. I tell the kids in The Learner's Lab that in regular question-answer (closed-question) thinking, their brains are like rulers going from one end to the other, but when they tackle open-ended questions or I ask them to think creatively, I want them to use their brain like a rubber band – stretch it and twist it and turn it inside out.

Their minds expand, their understanding deepens, and they begin to see the connections between seemingly unrelated things. It's a journey of discovery that never loses its thrill.

The Best Thing. . .

I love writing in curly cursive. I enjoy math and science a lot because they are fun.

—Sloane, 7

Your kiddo learns to approach information with a discerning eye, to question and dissect it, and to arrive at their own conclusions. This skill, honed through open-ended questions, is the foundation of wise decision-making. The best questions come from active listening, and engaging with your child, their thoughts, worries, or even the things they're studying, but sometimes a parent just needs something to get the conversation started. Here are 125 open-ended questions and conversation starters to get the dialogue going:

- Are there any other possibilities?
- Describe a happy memory that you have.
- Describe a memorable experience you have had with your family.
- Describe an act of kindness someone once showed you.
- Describe an act of kindness you performed this week for someone.
- Describe an instance when you did something foolish.
- Describe something you consistently forget to do.
- Describe the earliest thing you can recall about your parents or siblings.
- Describe the most amazing thing you've ever witnessed.
- Describe the quality about your best friend that you like best.
- Describe the type of store you'd own if you opened one.
- Describe what you enjoy most about summer.
- Describe what you enjoy most about the winter.
- Describe which family activities you would like to do more of.
- Describe your current goals.
- Describe your ideal treehouse.
- Did you laugh or smile more today? What caused you to laugh?
- Did you learn anything new from this? What?

- Do you ever have recurring thoughts? Describe them.
- Do you have a favorite time of year, food, place, or person?
- Do you have any ideas for inventions? Describe them.
- Do you have any ideas about . . .?
- Do you have any other suggestions? If so, what are they?
- Explain why that happened.
- Have you ever had an imaginary friend? Describe them to me.
- How could we improve . . .?
- How could you . . .?
- How did that come about?
- How did you learn so much about it?
- How did you think of that answer?
- How do you feel about . . .?
- How many hugs do you need each day?
- How would you define *intelligence*?
- How would you introduce yourself to someone if they had never met you?
- How would you sum up your week?
- I'm curious how . . . .
- Can you explain that further for me?
- If you could change one thing, then what would happen?
- If you had a different name, what would it be? Why?
- If you won a million dollars, what would you do? Then what?
- If you wrote a book, what would it be about?
- Imagine you were a chef; describe your restaurant to me. What kinds of food would you serve?
- Name a person you can trust. What about that person inspires trust?
- Now describe a time when . . .
- Tell me a new word you learned. What does it mean?
- Tell me about the best and worst parts of your day.
- Tell me about your favorite movie/TV show/YouTube series.
- Tell me how . . . .
- Tell me more, please . . . .
- This week, are you struggling with anything academically? How can I help?
- What about that did you like?
- What about this place do you like best/least?
- What about you do you believe I may not be aware of?
- What about your family do you love the most? Why?
- What activities do you enjoy the most?

- What activities would you engage in if you were going to spend the full day outside?
- What animal, if any, would you choose to be, and why?
- What are you currently thinking about?
- What are you interested in learning about? Why?
- What are you most proud of? Why?
- What brings you joy?
- What can you do to make it a wonderful day?
- What would be your dream vacation and why? How do you plan to get there?
- What characteristics define a good friend?
- What chore do you enjoy doing the most? Which do you dislike the most? Why?
- What color best represents happiness? Why?
- What do I do for you that you find comforting and loving?
- What do you dislike? Why?
- What do you hope to accomplish in life?
- What do you like to do the most to unwind after a busy day?
- What do you like to give to others?
- What do you see?
- What do you suppose might happen next?
- What do you think will happen next?
- What do you think led up to this?
- What do you want to collect? Why?
- What does a great day look like to you?
- What does it feel like to be hugged by someone?
- What does that feel like to you?
- Which four words best describe you?
- Which game do you prefer to play? Why?
- What gave you the idea?
- What gives you energy?
- What has been the best thing to happen to you? Why?
- What inspires you to be brave?
- What inspires you to feel gratitude?
- What inspires you to love?
- What irritates you the most?
- What is another approach we could try?
- What is one thing you would never sell? Why?
- What is something that really cheers you up?
- What is the funniest expression you can muster? How did you learn to do that?
- What is your greatest dream?
- What kind of weather do you like best? Why?
- What led to that?
- What makes you a great person?

- What musical genres do you prefer, and why?
- What one thing could you do all day long without becoming bored?
- What part did you prefer?
- What properties of it would you change?
- What characteristics make a bad friend?
- What should go here?
- What should you do if you witness unfair treatment of someone?
- What sound irritates you the most? Why?
- What three wishes, if any, would you most like to have granted? Why?
- What was the best gift you have ever gotten? What set it apart?
- What was the funniest thing you saw this week? Why?
- What was the hardest thing you ever had to deal with, and how did you get through it?
- What was the silliest thing you ever did? Why?
- What will happen if we change this?
- What would happen if . . .?
- What would improve it?
- What would you tell a friend if they told you to keep a secret that made you uncomfortable?
- What would you like to say to your younger self? Why?
- When people glare at you, what do you do?
- When you feel most like yourself, what are you doing?
- When you wake up, what do you think of first?
- When you're scared, what do you do? How does that help?
- Where would you be if you could be anyplace right now?
- Which action would you take?
- Which book, if any, would you keep if you could only keep one? Why?
- Which cereal is your favorite? Why?
- Which fictional character do you most identify with?
- Which language would you choose to learn? Why?

Setting the Stage

I walked into the kitchen one winter morning to find Logan and Isaac deep in concentration at the table. Glancing at the pile of tiny clay food waiting for me to bake, I realized they'd been up for a while. My youngest two have always been early risers, and I am decidedly not. One of my favorite things about homeschooling is that it allows us to find our own rhythms and schedules, and since I do my best work late into the night, we start a little later than some. Early on, I realized that, in order to have a cup or two of hot coffee in peace each morning, I'd need to make sure there was something engaging and meaningful for my kids to do before we started our official day. It would be even better if it was something that could spark creativity and encourage independent learning.

We're pretty eclectic when it comes to our homeschooling, as you've undoubtedly picked up as you've read this book. I especially enjoy the freedom homeschoolers have to pick and choose pieces of various styles of teaching, making them our own. One of those strategies I still use with my teens is strewing. The term *strewing* was first coined by Sandra Dodd, author of *Sandra Dodd's Big Book of Unschooling*. Strewing is a sanity-saver and a wonderful tool to have in your arsenal for sparking curiosity, learning, imagination, and creativity.

I have very bright kiddos. To keep them out of trouble while I'm still waking up, I used this idea and started setting out things for them to discover in the morning. In the preceding anecdote, I had set out a small cookie sheet that was reserved for baking crafts when necessary, clay in various colors, and plastic tools. Strewing involves placing intriguing things around your home so your children can discover them. These things can be anything that may inspire learning, creativity, or wonder. Kids have an innate curiosity that sparks a need to explore their world. As homeschoolers, our goal is to encourage this interest.

When you strew something for your kids to discover, you're rolling out the red carpet for your child's imagination. You're giving them the tools and materials to dive into possibilities. They get to call the shots, make choices, and act independently. In other words, they become the architects of their own learning journey. It's not just about having a good time – it's about building self-confidence. Your child learns to control their own motivation, behavior, and social interactions. They become fearless explorers, unafraid of trying, failing, and trying again. It's a journey of self-discovery and personal growth. Plus, strewing strengthens your child's autonomy and inner drive, all while teaching essential life skills like setting goals, negotiating, and sharing ideas. It's low-pressure learning by doing.

One of the things my kids like most about the things I strew is the element of surprise. And your child will too. They get to initiate their exploration, which taps into the motivation of novelty and unexpected discoveries. They learn from their mistakes, they take risks, and they let their creativity soar. Best of all, this nurtures their love of learning and lays a strong foundation for academic and social success.

The Best Thing. . .

I get to learn in ways I understand.

—Aberdeen, 9

Loose parts are great to set out when your kids are younger because they're so open-ended. You provide materials like shells, pinecones, or stones, and your child can count them, weigh them, sort them, play games with them, or use them in art. The possibilities are endless. And, you don't need to be the expert guiding every step. Your kiddos are invited to think and explore, and the direction is entirely up to them. It's like a canvas, and they're the artists.

It's important to remember not to hold too tightly to the things you strew. Your goal is to spark curiosity and let the kids run with it. You'll set yourself up for disappointment as a parent if you're putting something out as the start of a new unit study or because you think your kids need a bit more practice in an area. Strewing fails when we get caught up in a desired outcome. If I strew space stuff – a book, games, maybe queue a video on the computer, and put out some space toys – but the kids find a book about Ancient Egypt on the shelf and dive into that instead, it might feel like I've failed. And I did if I set out to start a unit study on space with them. But, when I keep in mind that strewing is about sparking curiosity, and not product placement, I realize that the Ancient Egypt play and conversation the kids are now involved in is a huge win. They're owning their learning, and it's a natural part of their lifestyle.

When it comes to strewing, the key is to strike a balance between allowing your child to discover and explore while keeping things tidy. No one wants a giant mess, right? To achieve this, consider limiting the number of items you strew each day. In fact, having too much clutter can make the strewing process more challenging. Don't get too hung up on time limits when it comes to strewing, either. It's crucial to give your kiddos the space and time they need to interact with these items. Let their imaginations run wild as they explore what you've set out for them.

Remember to keep it simple; don't spend a lot of money or time. Spending excessive time planning for strewing kind of defeats the purpose, right? Use a mix of items you already have on hand and easy-to-access materials. And, you don't have to strew every day. It's fun to see your children engaging with new things and learning independently through exploration, but there's no need to do it daily. I like to set up strewing opportunities two to four times a week, and I don't pressure myself to swap out items too quickly. If your kiddo is enjoying a particular collection, it's perfectly fine to leave it out for a few days. Don't overthink it.

Anytime you set out something engaging for your kiddos to discover, it's a total win. Even if it's a last-minute grab off the shelf and shove toward the kiddos before a meltdown ensues. You're working toward giving them autonomy over their learning and the knowledge that they *can* learn all they want to; they just need the right tools. Pull a forgotten game off the shelf and get down on the floor with the kids. Queue up a documentary on Amazon Prime, Netflix, or Curiosity Stream, and pop some popcorn, curl up on the couch, and watch something together – strewing *ideas* is just as important as strewing stuff. Documentaries are the perfect lazy-day strewing and can lead to amazing conversations. We watched a documentary a few years ago called *The Origami Code*, all about how the art of origami and the *folds* found in nature can lead us to amazing genetic discoveries. It was fascinating. Much of it was over the younger two kids' heads, but they folded paper happily when big sis led them in origami class while I was making lunch. My oldest, a teen at the time, was amazed and spent the better part of the afternoon looking things up online and comparing things he found to information that he'd read in his biology text. And he talked my ear off all that evening.

Sometimes it's fun to have a plan and pull things together beforehand. You may have an idea of something your kids would like, maybe basing it off a field trip coming up, a kit you have languishing in the cupboard, a class they've taken at co-op, or a conversation you overheard. You could pull books, toys, games, or an activity out for them to discover. I remember once, I knew there was a talk the kids would love coming up at our favorite nature center. Before I went to bed I set out the trays we keep on hand for messy activities and experiments, plastic forceps, skewers, a few owl and forest habitat books, and foil-wrapped owl pellets along with an identification chart. The kids loved it, compared finds, and then we snuggled on the couch to read the books and watch an owl documentary on Curiosity Stream. They were still interested in owls over the next few days, so we went to the nature center for the talk, checked out some more owl books from the library, wrote owl stories, and did some owl crafts. It was a blast.

But it's not always like that. Remember that strewing is a lot like setting the stage, and sometimes, it results in a standing ovation, and days and days of learning, and sometimes, it all falls flat. That's okay. Your job is to expose your kiddos to lots of great opportunities. Here are some simple ideas to get you started:

Books	Leave a variety of books around the house, covering different genres and subjects. You can include both fiction and nonfiction books.
Art Supplies	Set up an art station with a variety of art supplies, such as sketchbooks, colored pencils, watercolors, and clay. Encourage your child to explore their creativity.
Science Experiments	Provide science experiment kits or simple materials like baking soda and vinegar for at-home experiments.
Nature Exploration	Keep binoculars, a magnifying glass, and field guides handy for impromptu nature walks and birdwatching.
Maps and Globes	Place maps and globes around your home to encourage geography exploration and discussions.
Puzzles and Brain Teasers	Offer jigsaw puzzles, Sudoku books, or other brain-teasing games for critical thinking and problem-solving.
Musical Instruments	Leave musical instruments like a keyboard, guitar, or a set of drums available for your child to experiment with.
Educational Games	Board games and card games with educational elements can be strewn to make learning fun.

(continued)

Collections	Encourage your child to start a collection, whether it's rocks, stamps, coins, or something else that interests them.
Cooking and Baking	Set up a child-friendly cooking or baking station with simple recipes and ingredients.
Historical Artifacts	Display artifacts, replicas, or photographs from different historical periods to spark an interest in history.
Inspirational Quotes	Place inspiring quotes or thought-provoking questions around the house for your child to discover and ponder.
Museum and Zoo Memberships	Use memberships to local museums, zoos, or science centers to make spontaneous field trips.
Field Guides	Keep field guides on subjects like birds, insects, plants, or animals to encourage outdoor exploration and learning.
Astronomy Tools	Invest in a telescope or star chart for astronomy enthusiasts to explore the night sky.
Documentaries and Educational Videos	Leave out DVDs or streaming services with educational documentaries and series for your child to watch.
Foreign Language Resources	Incorporate foreign language learning by providing language apps, books, or online courses.
Board Books and Learning Toys	For younger children, include educational board books and toys that promote fine motor skills and early learning.
STEM Kits	Provide STEM (Science, Technology, Engineering, and Math) kits or materials to nurture an interest in these subjects.
Themed Learning Stations	Create themed learning stations in your home with hands-on activities related to a specific topic.

The Best Thing. . .

I liked customizing the classes I wanted to
take and having autonomy within those classes
themselves, like how I was able to choose the
books I wanted to read for my English credits.
—Drew, 19

Remember that the key to successful strewing is to allow your child the freedom to explore these materials at their own pace and to follow their interests. By providing a stimulating and enriching environment, you can foster a love for learning and help your child become more self-motivated in their homeschooling journey.

Try This!

- **Creativity can be taught:** Challenge the misconception that creativity is innate by teaching creative thinking skills. Integrate creative thinking exercises into your child's learning, such as using analogies, metaphors, and visual thinking to solve problems.
- **The Torrance framework for creative thinking:** Utilize the four components (fluency, flexibility, originality, elaboration) to nurture creativity in your child. Create activities that emphasize each component, such as brainstorming sessions for fluency and exploring multiple solutions for flexibility.
- **Questioning fosters imagination:** Show your child that open-ended questions lead to self-expression and independent thought. Model curiosity by asking your child open-ended questions about their interests and experiences.
- **Transitioning from closed-ended to open-ended questions:** Gradually introduce open-ended questions and discuss their importance in fostering deeper conversations.
- **The element of surprise:** Use strewing to ignite your child's sense of novelty and curiosity. Occasionally introduce unexpected materials or experiences to pique your child's interest.

- **Be open to surprises:** Encourage your child's curiosity and interests, even if they deviate from your initial plans.
- **Strewing principles:** Provide your child with the freedom to explore, make choices, and act independently through strewing. Offer a variety of materials, such as loose parts like shells or stones, to inspire your child's curiosity and learning.
- **Simplicity in strewing:** Keep the process straightforward and focus on sparking your child's curiosity, rather than overthinking it. Use readily available materials and don't invest excessive time in planning strewing activities.
- **Variety in strewing:** Rotate strewn items to maintain your child's interest and adapt to their changing preferences.

8 | Embracing Adventure

The biggest adventure you can take is to live the life of your dreams.
—Oprah Winfrey

The world is not in your books and maps, it's out there.
—From *The Hobbit* by J.R.R. Tolkien

We left the dentist office and merged onto the highway. Three of the four kids sat in the backseat, reading or dozing; it had been a long appointment. My oldest sat in the passenger seat up front, and looked out the window, puzzled. "Where are we going?" he asked. "This isn't the way home." The others swiveled their heads quizzically to look out their windows and started talking at once.

"Relax," I said. "It's time for a Surprise Ride." Immediately, the guesses started, but I simply turned up the music. "I'm not telling, so settle in for the drive." A Surprise Ride could mean anything, so the kids spent the drive whispering, looking out the window to try and guess our direction, and throwing out predictions. These adventures started when Trevor was a few years old. I'd hop up, declare it was time for a Surprise Ride, and we'd go off on a journey of some sort. Some adventures were small, like a trip to a dollar store, the zoo where we had a membership, or the local park for

137

a picnic. Other times, the adventures were big, like this one. On the day of the dentist visit, I had packed overnight bags and booked the five of us on a midweek homeschool days special at Kalahari Resort in Sandusky, Ohio. We had three days and two nights to play in the arcade and swim in the indoor water park, and have the place pretty much to ourselves since it was a Tuesday during the school year.

Adventures like this give us a chance to use the flexibility homeschool offers to our advantage. It's much easier for homeschool families to switch around their schedules, bring work along on an overnight trip, or take time off in the middle of the week to take advantage of deals and empty venues. And they strengthen family relationships and build memories.

My friend Sarah Mackenzie, author of *Teaching From Rest* and *The Read Aloud Family*, calls these just-because-we-can days. We do things just because we can, too. We start school later in the day, take lots of breaks, and go to the zoo in the middle of the week. I try to sprinkle in Surprise Rides, big and small, to shake up things, have some fun, and keep the kids guessing. Adventures bring families together, help kids feel safe and loved, and create a shared history filled with stories. All worth taking time for.

The Best Thing. . .

When you're homeschooled, you can enjoy fun things when there are no crowds. You can spend more time with your family too. Going on family trips is a great way to relax and unwind.

—Jayden, 14

Going on adventures with our kids can offer lots of educational advantages that go beyond the limitations of a conventional classroom. Children who participate in outdoor activities are exposed to so much, developing a profound respect for the natural world and its ecological processes. Being outside requires physical effort, which improves kids' physical health and well-being. When kids explore new settings and circumstances, the obstacles they face and overcome facilitate critical thinking and problem-solving abilities. Adventures ignite curiosity, which feeds a love of learning and provides independence in acclimating to unfamiliar surroundings, boosting confidence. Through exploring with their families, kids can improve spatial awareness and build resilience. Kids get the chance to learn about species, ecosystems, the workings of the world, and scientific ideas. A fascination with history and cultural heritage is sparked by seeing historical locations during adventures, which provide insights into the past. All things considered, going on adventures cultivates a spirit of adventure, a positive outlook on life, an acceptance of difficulties, and a lifetime love of discovery and education. So, beyond the fun, just-because-we-can days and Surprise Rides boost our kids learning in immeasurable ways!

Experiences Big and Small

What started as an enjoyable way to have some fun with my little guy turned into a much-loved tradition. We took Surprise Rides, but we also adventured together as often as we could. When I first started homeschooling, Trevor was six, Molly was three, and Logan was an infant. I'd been freelancing from home as an education writer since Molly was born and knew it would be easy to fall into the box-checking mode working and homeschooling parents can easily fall prey to. I didn't want it to be all about homeschool, work, and housework. I wanted fun, too. As a neurodivergent mom raising neurodivergent kids, we have loads of challenges that can all be regulated by keeping things novel, adding in the unexpected, getting outside, moving as much as possible, and doing things our brains find interesting. I decided that we would get out of the house every day for at least a short while, even if it was only to take a walk around the neighborhood.

Our adventuring began. We took long walks, short ones, climbed trees, visited parks, went to bounce house places, visited the library, had ice cream for lunch, or took advantage of the science center, zoo, and botanical garden memberships I'd purchased. Some of our adventures were Surprise Rides; others were planned and chosen by the kids. Just today, as I'm writing this book, Isaac came in my office to tell me that he's craving apple cider. It's fall here in Ohio, and the day is gorgeous: blue skies filled with puffy, white clouds, the sun filtering through those clouds, highlighting the brightly colored leaves on the trees, and the crisp, cool air. The kids played outside much of the day because fall is the best time of the year here. I completely understand the craving for cider, so instead of working in the morning and afternoon tomorrow as planned, we're going to take off on an adventure to our favorite farm, grab some pumpkin donuts and apple cider for breakfast, pick pumpkins and apples, grab a few gallons of cider, and some brightly colored mums to plant in front of the house. Some fresh air, fall treats, and a little break in routine will do all of us good. Going on adventures, big and small, is great for the whole family.

Rarely are the activities themselves especially distinctive or spectacular. But the outing becomes more interesting by giving it a unique name, like Adventure Day or Surprise Ride. We made the choice to team up and brainstorm ideas that we could keep on hand for when we need inspiration. We began compiling a list of all the free or low-cost activities available in the area. There were large and small ones. Some were activities, while others were places. I listed some locations that were close by and some that were a little farther away. There are a ton of alternatives. When we want an Adventure Day, we aim to rotate through them.

On Adventure Days and Surprise Rides, I put away my cellphone. Okay, I do pull it out here and there to take pictures, but I don't check email, social media, or do any work. The kids get my attention. I truly exist in the moment with my children, which means more to them than I ever expected. These adventures are all the more special because of the undivided attention that we give to each other. It's not really about the activity we do together as much as the connections we build.

Keeping It Simple and Purposeful

Remember to keep it simple. We tend to think that family adventures must be elaborate events. However, a trip doesn't have to be spectacular to count as an adventure. A small change can have a significant effect. Particularly, when it is carried out with love and purpose. Greta Eskridge, author of *Adventuring Together: How to Create Connections and Make Lasting Memories with Your Kids*, says, "adventure is the vehicle, but connection is the goal." Your child is going to follow your lead if you're engaged and enjoying yourself. Therefore, your kids will have more fun when you have fun. The absolute best kind of modeling!

The Best Thing. . .

I enjoy homeschooling because I can pick and choose what I want to learn, work at my own pace, and make friends, which I never had the chance to do in public school. Getting to know other homeschoolers is also fun for me because they get why it works.

—Peyton, 16

While I can truly say I am grateful for the times I tune into the adventure and stay present, it takes practice. Cut yourself a break if you get distracted from time to time. Our kiddos know how to have fun; it's we adults who need to relearn it sometimes. Adventures don't have to be expensive, involve extensive planning, or demand expensive equipment. Some of our best Adventure Days and Surprise Rides are the ones that came up naturally when I said yes to one of the kids' ideas.

One of our recent Adventure Days will be remembered forever – or go down in infamy. We took an impromptu hike on the beach through the marsh trail and over the dunes. It was just Logan, Isaac, and me, as the older two were away that day. The weather was perfect, and though we hadn't brought swimsuits, we took off our shoes and waded in the water, grabbing wave-polished rocks and sea glass that sparkled up at us. Isaac, being a ten-year-old boy, "accidentally" fell in the water, and since he was already wet, I just let him dive and splash. When he was tired of the water, we made our way back, and found a perfectly intact, and rather large, fish skull. Despite their protests, Isaac grabbed a stick for me, while Logan held open a plastic bag. I picked up the fish skull with the stick and put it in the bag.

My kiddos were a little disgusted but resigned as their strange home-school mama had collected things from hikes before. We had a blast making our way back to the van, using our app to identify plants on the way. When we arrived home, I put the fish skull in a large pot to boil off the remaining skin, and, um, other stuff so we could look at the clean skull using the digital microscope we have for our desktop computer. And here's where the day took a little turn. You see, I don't have a sense of smell. It's one of those weird, quirky facts about me that not everyone knows. I probably did have a sense of smell at some point, but I suffered from so many recurring sinus issues when I was young, and underwent multiple sinus surgeries over the course of more than a decade, that I can't remember ever smelling anything. While I boiled the fish head, my kids deserted me and went outside. I didn't think anything of it until my husband got home with Molly and they both gagged as soon as they came in.

Apparently, what I was doing by boiling the fish head was permeating every corner of the house with rotting fish scent. The house reeked and made it impossible for anyone to be inside. I was completely unaware that anything was wrong. My husband grabbed the pot off the stove, poured the water deep in the woods, and hosed off the now clean skull. I went around the house and opened all the windows to air out everything.

Trusting the Process

While my method of cleaning a fish skull was not the best, we did see some pretty cool details looking at it through the digital microscope. And, while everyone was fascinated by the way the teeth and cartilage looked, they still tease me about it today and probably will for the rest of my life. What makes adventures truly extraordinary is their incredible power to inspire connection. Adventures take us away from our everyday routines and give us energy. Changing things up allows us to see things from new perspectives. We find new places to explore, try new restaurants, discover pieces of nature we'd never known before, and more.

I love finding things to explore with my kids. Experiencing the world around us together takes us out of our normal, making sure we don't get into the rut that homeschool can easily become. Instead, we become fully immersed in the world and in each other. My kids are cool people. They're the absolute best companions for me to spend time with, and that time is so well spent. I want them to engage in the world around them, make eye contact with people they meet, start up conversations, ask questions when they don't know answers, notice the birds, the clouds, the trickle of water from a stream up ahead on the trail. I bet you want this for your kids, too.

Homeschooling with a child focus, with the goal of raising lifelong lovers of learning, means that we need to be present, trust that the time invested is worth it, and make sure we're engaged, welcoming, and willing to admit our own mistakes to solve problems together. We must channel our time, energy, and attention into nurturing our children's lives.

Embracing the idea of Adventure Days and Surprise Rides isn't always easy, though. It requires dedication, not only to start but also to persevere through discomfort and adversity. When Isaac interrupted my work to tell me he was craving apple cider, I could have easily brushed it off, told him there was orange juice in the refrigerator, or opened up my grocery delivery app and put it on the list. Instead, I recognized that he wasn't really asking for cider. He associates cider with our fall farm trips, and what he was really craving was time with me out of the house. Writing a book is a lot of work, and when I get deep into a project, especially near its due date, I tend to hole up in my office, serve frozen meals or take-out for dinner, and do the bare minimum around the house. I always laugh, particularly when I'm deep into a big project, at the idea that most of us homeschool parents are looking for balance and beating ourselves up when we can't find it. The truth is that there is no balance. Instead, like a picky toddler who eats his way through the week, some days a lot and other days barely anything, it all evens out over time. Sometimes I spend a tremendous amount of time on a work project. Other times, I neglect work and play with my kids all day long for weeks. Isaac wants connection in the form of apple cider on a fall morning, so I'll take a few hours away from the book and play in the sun with the kids.

The Best Thing. . .

The best thing about being homeschooled
was the relationships I formed with my family.
Through the adventures, stories, and time we
shared together, my mom and my siblings became
some of my dearest friends.

—Audrey, 22

When I first started taking the kids on Adventure Days and Surprise Rides, I looked like a pack mule. I was laden down with coolers, snacks, water bottles, changes of clothes, and had more in my van just in case. But I was committed to doing things differently than the school system had done. I wanted connection over correction, adventurous spirits, and to build strong, confident, resilient kids who truly enjoyed each other. While often exhausting, I know that it was worth it. Just the other night, when my fourteen-year-old's rehearsal was canceled and the kids (21, 16, 14, and 10) realized they were all home together with nothing going on that night or the next morning, they came together to pop popcorn and have a movie marathon on the couch, making sure the ten-year-old was included and that the movie was fun for all, but appropriate for him.

I remind myself often that, if life goes the way it should, those kids will have each other long after I'm gone. I want them to build strong enough relationships now that can become the foundation for future bonds that last a lifetime. I want them to visit each other on college campuses. I want them to be there to support one another through births and deaths and sickness and health. These simple adventures can help plant a root system those future relationships can grow from.

Nurturing Resilience and Imagination

There's more, though. Taking adventures with your kids benefits them socially, emotional, physically, and academically, too. When you step outside, nature becomes your classroom, and every hike, camping trip, or visit to a local park is an opportunity for learning. Homeschooling allows you the flexibility to adapt your curriculum to the seasons, weather, and outdoor resources. Isaac's craving for cider and connection time stemmed from annual trips to the farm. In his mind, it's just something we do during the fall. As you venture outdoors, your kids can learn about ecosystems, weather patterns, local wildlife, and even navigation, all while developing a sense of wonder and respect for the environment.

Adventure encourages kids to ask questions, seek answers, and explore the unknown. Whether it's gazing at the stars on a clear night, asking a museum volunteer for information, finding new species of pumpkins at the farm, or identifying tracks of animals in the snow, every adventure sparks curiosity. It's this curiosity that will drive your kiddos to spend their lives seeking knowledge and understanding of the world around them, making learning a natural and exciting part of their lives. When we went to the farm, there were dozens of apple species, many I'd never heard of. Since it wasn't crowded, the owner was able to take time with Isaac and me, and told us how the different species came to be, what each was good for, as some were better for baking or cooking, others were good for sauces, and still others were best for eating. Then she took one of each type and let us taste them all. Isaac saw me asking questions to learn more about the apples I'd never heard of, and my hope is that he'll remember that it's okay to not know things and ask questions when you don't. If an old lady like his mama can say she doesn't know, and find someone who does, then so can he. These incredible life lessons pop up all the time when you let yourself adventure with your kids and lean in to the freedom homeschooling allows.

The Best Thing. . .

It makes me happy that my mom teaches me.

—Michael, 5

Taking your kids on adventures gives them loads of opportunities for hands-on learning. Cooking over a campfire teaches them chemistry and patience. Checking out a living history location gives them a chance to see how life was in a different time. Setting up a tent hones problem-solving skills. Visiting a behind-the-scenes tour lets them experience how a product is made. We loved the chocolate and whistle factory tours we've gone on – so cool! Identifying edible plants cultivates practical knowledge. Even something as simple as visiting a library allows for hands-on learning as they navigate the overwhelming selection of books and resources, then choose just the right one. These skills not only help them academically, but also prepare them for real-life situations.

One of my favorite things about adventuring together as a family is that it deepens our bonds. It creates shared memories and experiences that form the foundation of a strong, communicative relationship. Conversations around the campfire, discussing plants and animals you see, and collaborating to decide where you'll go and what you'll do, all promote open communication, problem-solving, and teamwork. It also gives you shared stories that bring you together as you reminisce around the dinner table long after the experience. My kids still talk about the road trip we took from Ohio to California when I was invited to speak at a conference out there one summer. We decided to take a few weeks to drive there, hopping on and off Route 66, stopping to see some of the most famous sights along the way. Before we left, we spent time looking at maps, with each kiddo choosing a place they most wanted to see based on descriptions and tourist reviews. Once we had our stops in place, my oldest helped my husband find hotels along the route, and we piled all we needed, along with the six of us, into the minivan and headed out.

It wasn't the most perfect trip you could ever hope for. One of the hotels we'd booked was falling apart and not safe to stay at, so we had to find other accommodations after a too-long travel day. On the way back, there was a blackout one night in the city we'd stayed in, and nobody had gotten any sleep that night in the un-air-conditioned three-digit heat, so we stayed another night and explored the city so we didn't drive while exhausted. But there were amazing points, too. The kids loved the Blue Whale of Catoosa in Catoosa, Oklahoma, a concrete whale a man named Hugh Davis built for his wife as a gift for their 34th wedding anniversary in 1972. We also had a blast spray painting the cars at Cadillac Ranch in Amarillo, Texas. So much fun, and the mishaps just made the memories so much more enjoyable to talk about years later.

Going on adventures big and small gives you a chance to expose your kids to cultural and historical experiences. My friend Jessica and her family have spent countless hours on the road visiting national parks throughout the country. Through these visits and trips, they've learned about the cultural significance of different landforms and monuments; the geography of our country; and have learned about geology, history, and the plants and animals found in different regions. They'll remember more about history, culture, and science than they would have if they'd sat in a classroom reading books about these topics. Visiting historical sites, exploring different regions, and interacting with local communities can teach your kids about traditions, history, and customs firsthand.

The physical aspect of getting out and adventuring is crucial in today's age of screens and sedentary lifestyles. Regular outdoor activities build strong bodies and minds. Additionally, overcoming challenges, facing fears, and developing resilience on adventures are vital emotional skills that can't be learned from books alone. One of my son's best friends from the neighborhood where we lived when he was young didn't get outside that often. His parents both worked and his dad struggled with anxiety, and as a result, preferred the kids play either inside or on the playground set he had in the backyard with its cushiony foam mulch edged in beneath it. Trevor preferred to swing from our monkey bars, ride his bike without a helmet, and climb trees. Carlos wasn't allowed to climb with him, but he was always there to cheer him on. One afternoon, though, Carlos decided that it was time he learned to climb a tree like the other neighborhood kids, and Trevor set out to help him. They chose a tree in our yard, just out of my line of vision through the kitchen window and far enough away from Carlos's house that his dad wouldn't catch sight of the adventure either.

Apparently, it went well at first. Carlos and Trevor chose the tree, not just for its distance and location just out of sight, but because it had a V in the trunk, which they thought would give the newbie tree climber an added boost to be able to brace his feet on if he needed it. And it did, until he started slipping. Carlos panicked as he climbed higher and started slipping down the left fork of the trunk, and as he slid faster, he tried to bring his legs up to help grab onto the trunk and slow his descent. Instead, his bent knee met the point of the V where the two trunks joined back into one with the full weight of his body and force of his panicked slide. He jammed his knee into that spot with such intensity that it was wedged in so snugly he was suspended from that knee several feet off the ground and couldn't get out.

The Best Thing. . .

I can choose what to learn. I am free to grow in any way I choose. I don't have to take tests that make me feel dumb.

                                        —Miles, 14

Of course, I didn't see any of this. This was told to me after Trevor calmly walked into the kitchen, grabbed a couple of juice boxes out of the refrigerator, and asked if I could come out and help because Carlos was stuck in the tree. Not particularly worried, I headed outside expecting to see a nervous ten-year-old boy who had climbed his first tree too high, and was scared to climb back down. Instead, I found Carlos literally stuck IN the tree, his knee bent and wedged between the split trunks, a chair under his other leg to take some of the pressure, playing Trevor's Nintendo DS.

It seems that after Trevor had realized that Carlos wasn't hurt, and that he couldn't get him out of the tree himself, he decided to make his friend comfortable before tracking me down, so he'd gotten him a chair from the yard and the game to keep him occupied. Being used to mishaps on the trail and things going wrong while out and about, Trevor tried solving the problem himself, and when he couldn't, he made his friend comfortable and asked for help.

Creativity often flourishes in adventurous and outdoor settings. Your kiddos can draw inspiration from the world around them, whether it's sketching a sunset, writing a journal, composing a poem, or pulling up a chair so Carlos wasn't hanging by his knee. Adventure nurtures their imagination and encourages them to express themselves and solve problems.

Adventuring with kids is not just beneficial for homeschooling families, it is an integral part of a well-rounded education. It fosters curiosity, hands-on learning, life skills, bonding, cultural understanding, physical and emotional growth, creative expression, and personalized learning.

And Carlos made it out of the tree. I had to go break the news to his dad, who fought his way through the panic-attack brought on as soon as he saw his son dangling in the tree. I helped him through it, assuring him that his son was unhurt, while Trevor and Carlos shared the snack my son had made and brought outside. In the end, he was just wedged in too tightly for us to free him, so we had to call the fire department. The responding fire fighters stood around for a long time, trying to wrap their heads around one of the most unusual calls they'd ever been to. Human force could not pry those trunks apart enough for Carlos to slip his knee out, so they ended up strapping a helmet to his head and using a tool on the "jaws of life" that inflated to lift objects off victims. They pushed the limbs apart until he slid out into his father's arms. Carlos's knee had imprints from his jeans, similar to the creases you get on your face when you sleep too hard on a folded blanket. Other than that, he was fine.

Try This!

- **Create adventure traditions:** Initiate fun and memorable traditions like Adventure Days or Surprise Rides to bond with your children.
- **Maintain novelty:** Regularly introduce new experiences to keep things interesting and engaging for neurodivergent children. Explore

various activities and places like libraries, botanical gardens, and science centers.

- **Be present:** Give your children your full attention during adventures to build strong connections.
- **Keep it simple:** Remember that family adventures don't have to be elaborate; small changes can have a significant impact. A walk around the neighborhood can be just as valuable as an elaborate trip.
- **Model enjoyment:** Set an example by having fun during adventures; your kids will follow your lead.
- **Practice flexibility:** Embrace impromptu adventures and be open to your kids' ideas. Say yes to your kids' spontaneous adventure requests.
- **Plan and prepare:** Be ready for adventures by planning and packing accordingly. Prepare for outings with essentials like snacks, water, and extra clothes.
- **Strengthen sibling bonds:** Encourage strong relationships among your children through shared adventures. Organize movie nights or outings where each child has a say in the plans.
- **Engage in educational adventures:** Explore nature to teach your kids about ecosystems, weather, and local wildlife.
- **Encourage curiosity:** Foster a sense of wonder and a habit of asking questions during adventures. Together, identify plants, stars, or historical facts during outings.
- **Hands-on learning:** Adventures offer hands-on educational opportunities. Try cooking over a campfire to teach science and patience.
- **Promote open communication:** Encourage your children to communicate openly during adventures. Use campfire conversations to discuss what you've seen and learned.
- **Build memories:** Recall past trips and enjoy the connections formed during those adventures.
- **Learn about culture and history:** Explore cultural and historical sites during your adventures. Understand traditions, history, and customs by interacting with different regions.
- **Prioritize physical activity:** Counteract sedentary lifestyles by engaging in outdoor activities. Participate in physical challenges like hiking and camping.
- **Develop resilience:** Let children take calculated risks like climbing trees under supervision.

- **Foster creativity:** Adventures in natural settings stimulate creativity and problem-solving skills. Allow your kids to sketch, write, or compose during outdoor outings.
- **Teach empathy:** Encourage your children to show kindness and support during challenges. Model empathy and helping others.
- **Build lifelong bonds:** Plan memorable road trips, where kids have a say in the itinerary, to strengthen family ties.

9 | The Family Team

Family is not an important thing. It's everything.

—Michael J. Fox

On the night you were born, the moon smiled with such wonder that the stars peeked in to see you and the night wind whispered, "Life will never be the same."

—From *On the Night You Were Born* by Nancy Tillman

James and his dad shared a passion for gardening, turning it into a cherished hobby. Their journey began with late-night YouTube sessions, where they'd watch garden shows, learning the ropes of gardening from online experts. As their interest grew, they decided to delve into the world of potato cultivation, sparking a year-long project. Surprisingly, they managed to turn this into a high school botany credit without following any specific curriculum. Instead, they faithfully watched 40-minute YouTube gardening shows, absorbing knowledge about plant identification, soil types, and climate variations across the United States. Living in Florida, they ventured to garden shops to gather supplies and experimented with seed planting, nurturing, and propagating various plants.

This hobby soon transformed into a passion, offering James a unique approach to scientific learning. It took him outdoors, digging holes, setting up irrigation systems, and solving problems as they arose. His enthusiasm persisted, with him even drafting a list of vegetables to grow in the upcoming year. Beyond the garden, James assumed responsibility for yard maintenance, dealing with tasks like weeding and grass care. He began to contemplate the possibility of turning this skill into a side job. Their family also incorporated gardening into their travels, making it a point to visit botanical gardens nationwide. James's deep interest and knowledge allowed him to identify plants and trees with ease, showcasing the depth of his passion.

Reflecting on their journey, James's mom acknowledged the importance of nurturing his deep interests. Gifted kiddos like James crave in-depth knowledge, a concept she initially struggled to grasp. Yet, witnessing James's immersive exploration in gardening provided her with valuable insights. Allowing kids to become experts in their chosen fields, especially if they can do it alongside family, bolsters their confidence and fosters mutual learning. This dynamic relationship between parents and children isn't about exerting authority; it's a shared journey of discovery.

As homeschooling parents, you know that the relationship your children have with you is the most important one in their lives. This link between parents and children is essentially where your children's understanding of the world begins. They look to you as they mature and develop to determine how secure they feel and how much you love them. Their future interactions and connections are built on the fundamental foundation of this relationship.

The Best Thing. . .

I love that I get to hang out with and bond with
my family.

—Ariana, 10

In James's case, his shared gardening pursuit with his dad not only strengthened their bond, but also introduced an element of friendly competition. They enjoyed trips to Home Depot and garden shops together, and had lively debates about plant identification. Their yearly visit to Epcot's garden festival added an extra layer of excitement, as they used a plant identification app to test each other's knowledge. When kids take the initiative to learn on their own, it benefits not only their personal growth, but also enriches the whole family.

Growing Relationships

Here's the thing: kids are born to learn. Literally. Dr. Patricia Kuhl, I-Labs Co-Director at the University of Washington, explains that brain development begins before birth and continues throughout adulthood, but the most rapid development happens in the first three years of life. By age three, a child has three times more brain activity than an adult. The brain over-produces the synaptic connections it will need and becomes dense, remaining that way throughout the first decade of a child's life.

Dr. Kuhl says, "Brian development works in a way that these connections keep getting formed and they overproduce themselves. It's as though the brain is getting ready for everything, and so every neuron tries to connect with every other neuron, producing a brain with more connections than it really needs. So, the process of the brain is to over-proliferate these connections, then systematically prune the ones you don't use, that you don't need." It's our job as parents to help our kids as they go through that over-producing and pruning process.

I bet you're thinking, like so many of the parents she works with have thought, *But I don't want my baby's brain to prune.* Right? But, we do. We do want our children's brains to prune because, as Dr. Kuhl explains, "pruning in our kids' brains, like for a rose bush, will strengthen all the remaining connections. As it's pruned systematically, your child ends up with very strong stems, or strengths." Through this natural-born learning, our kids' brains become custom-designed to function in the environment they make for themselves.

And you get to shape that environment while growing strong relationships within your entire family.

When homeschooling, it's critical to be fully present with your children, spend quality time learning together, and create a space where they feel free to explore and express themselves. This will help to foster a strong parent-child relationship. The things is, there are no guarantees in parenting, so you'll likely fumble along the way. But, when you take the time to build the foundation for these relationships, you and your kids will bounce back more quickly every time.

Some of the most important things you can do to strengthen your relationships are the simplest to blend into your days. Here are my favorites:

- **Listen actively and show empathy:** The foundation of a strong relationship with your child is active listening. Acknowledge your child's feelings, demonstrate your understanding, and reassure them of your unwavering support. Strive to view the world from their perspective. Listening and empathizing not only solidify mutual respect, but also strengthen your parent-child bond.
- **Demonstrate your love:** Touch and affection are fundamental for healthy emotional and neurobiological development across all stages of life. Nurturing your child's emotional well-being requires a steady stream of gentle, loving gestures like hugs throughout the day. Every interaction should be viewed as an opportunity to foster connection. Begin by warmly greeting your child with eye contact, a sincere smile, and an invitation for open and honest communication.
- **Express your love verbally:** Telling our kids we love them is vital. Make it a daily habit, regardless of your child's age. Even when your child is having a difficult day and is behaving poorly, take time to reaffirm your unconditional love. It's these times your kids need the

most reassurance from you. A simple "I love you" holds the power to profoundly impact your long-term relationship with your child.

- **Eat together:** Family mealtimes are the perfect time for bonding and conversation with your child. Encourage everyone to stow away their phones and devices, focusing on the enjoyment of each other's company. These moments also offer a platform to instill the significance of a wholesome, balanced diet, which has a direct impact on their mental well-being.

- **Engage in play together:** Play is the gateway to your child's development. It serves as the canvas where they paint their language skills, express emotions, nurture creativity, and acquire vital social skills. It's also a fun way to strengthen your relationship with your child. What you play matters less than the quality time and undivided attention you invest in each other.

- **Establish boundaries:** Children thrive with structure and guidance as they explore the world around them. Engage your children in open conversations about your expectations. Take time to set up family standards and consequences together. When my kids were younger, we decided that our family's core value was kindness and everything stemmed from that. We let those values do the work for us, continually asking one another if what we were doing was kind, then problem-solving together. This fostered a sense of security and understanding, and made us a team.

- **Be present and free from distractions:** Reserve at least ten to fifteen minutes daily for uninterrupted conversations with each of your kiddos. Create a distraction-free zone by turning off the cellphones. This simple act underscores your child's importance in your life, demonstrating that they are a priority despite life's many distractions and stressors.

- **Create family rituals:** If you have multiple children, try to spend individual, quality time with each of them. These one-on-one moments bolster your relationship with each, boost your children's self-esteem, and convey their uniqueness and value. Consider scheduling special "date nights" with each child to create one-on-one opportunities, whether it's a stroll in the neighborhood, a trip to the playground, or a cozy movie night at home. Celebrating each child individually fortifies your bond.

The Best Thing. . .

I love the feeling of having extended family in the homeschool community. It's really cool that my best friend's mom is my science teacher!

—Tyler, 17

Remember, each parent–child relationship is different due to character traits, traditions, and more. One of your kids might crave cuddles when he's angry, while another might want to avoid hugs when she's upset. Follow your own judgment and that of the specific kiddo in front of you. You are the best parent for your child. Trust yourself.

Recognizing and Supporting Differences

When Logan was small, she had trouble falling asleep on her own. She has anxiety and sensory processing disorder, and one of the easiest ways for her to regulate was to have skin-to-skin contact. So I moved the big, cushiony recliner into the kids' room and held her on my lap, and rocked while her arm was tucked around my waist just under the hem of my shirt. She felt safe and loved, and I was able to take the time to decompress from the day and relax too.

At the time, she was the youngest, but the other two kids didn't feel left out because they weren't rocking with me every night before bed. One of them doesn't like being touched, so that would not have been comforting for her. She preferred to fall asleep listening to a story or music, snuggled into her big, fluffy blankets in a dimly lit room. The other just wanted to brain dump. He needed to tell someone everything he'd thought about or done throughout the day before he could clear his mind and go to sleep.

Each person brings something unique to the family dynamic. It's up to us to highlight each of the individual needs, strengths, weaknesses, and preferences so everyone understands everyone else. Our kids need to know they're part of a greater unit, and that what they bring to the table is valuable and needed. If we're to cultivate this team-like feeling within our home, we need to help each of our kids see the value the others bring. We need to wildly support one another.

For those of us with neurodivergent kiddos, this can feel more difficult. Remember, though, our children are who they're meant to be. We didn't do anything to cause a neurodivergence, and there are no mistakes, so it's up to us to tease out our kiddos' strengths and help them see the amazingness in themselves, while we show each member of the family how they fit into the greater whole. Whether your child is neurotypical or neurodivergent, they're exactly who your family needs to complete your whole.

It's important to stop fighting who our kids are and lean into them and their needs. If I'd subscribed to some parenting stances, I'd have left Logan in her bed, instituted a firm and early bedtime for Trevor, and told Molly she had to put her book away and turn the lights out completely at bedtime. Sure, they may have adjusted to those norms eventually, but I'd have damaged the trust they had for me and taught them to ignore their nervous systems' needs. Instead, I encourage you to lean into who your child is and what they need because things do get easier when our family is built on mutual love, trust, and a sense that we're a unit, a team.

Each member of our family team shares similarities. They all seem to come out of the womb with a very finely-honed sense of sarcastic humor.

Truly, there's nobody who can out-sarcasm my brood. It keeps a mom on her toes! The first and third born look like me, the second and fourth born look like my husband. They all enjoy staying up late into the night, and sleeping in for as long as possible. They enjoy movies, snacks, making messes, and trying to out-annoy one another.

The Best Thing. . .

I notice the kids in my neighborhood don't love learning as much as me and that's hard to understand because learning is fun. . . . It's probably not fun for them because they don't get to choose what they do.

—Lincoln, 12

But they have differences too. My oldest is the most outside-the-box person I know. He doesn't do anything in a conventional way and doubts his abilities and talents more than he trusts in himself. He's hard on others, and harder on himself. He's not taking a traditional route as he's entering adulthood and takes a two-steps-forward-one-step-back approach to just about everything he tries. Yet, despite his own doubt, he's taught classes to teens, works as a freelance audio and video editor, and is working toward getting both drone and real estate licenses.

My next born kiddo is smart, funny, articulate, and can read a person so accurately it's scary. I trust her opinions of people completely because she has a knack for seeing to the heart and through the mind of anyone. It's probably how she's able to tackle a new character so well. She's an incredible performer and plans to go on to study musical theater in college.

The third kiddo is sweet, sensitive, and worried all the time. She has such a deep well of empathy that I've often worried she'd be taken advantage of. She sees good in everyone, but doubts anyone sees good in her. She loves animals and can nurture just about any creature from the millipedes we have in a terrarium to the bearded dragon she received one Christmas to the dogs and chickens that seem to multiply around here. She wants to work with animals when she's grown.

My youngest keeps us all on our toes. He's funny, likes to cause mischief, has a bunch of energy, and has recently started dancing hip hop. He's the youngest by a lot, so that causes challenges sometimes, as having three older siblings with strong personalities can be overwhelming, but he's making his mark on the family. He loves all things video games, outside, and Nerf. We can't wait to see what he ends up doing.

Being a Family Team

Each of those kids brings something different to our family team, and each has strengths and weaknesses. It's up to us to help our kids see and celebrate the strengths in each other, while being there for their family members when they need support. When we're trying to build a team mentality in our families, it's important to make sure that each member celebrates the others. We have a few simple rules in our home, but the one that matters most, in my opinion, is that everyone who lives here needs to support each other in the things that they do. That means that each member of the family, even those who hate live theater, will attend at least one performance when a sibling is in a show. And, despite youth basketball being excruciating to watch when the kids are just learning, all family members go to at least one game each season. If there's a recital, art showing, film screening, musical, horse demonstration, or whatever, family shows up for family. When we support each other for the highs, it's easier and more natural to support each other for the lows.

The Best Thing. . .

I can play with my brother in between lessons!
—Sophie, 9

I remember being at a holiday party with the kids one year. They were scattered throughout the house with cousins and other guests, and I was in the kitchen talking with a few of the other adults. Isaac came up to me to let me know that Molly needed me in the room where we put our coats when I could get there. Once he delivered his message, he bounded off to play some more. When I got to the bedroom where we'd stowed our coats, I saw both my girls huddled in the corner, headphones on, a movie playing on the Kindle Fire, and Molly rubbing Logan's back in a rhythmic, swirling pattern. She smiled when she looked up and told me that Logan had gotten overwhelmed and needed a break, so she brought her to the room to take a sensory break. She wondered if I'd go get Logan some water, then stay with her a while longer so Molly could rejoin her cousins in the basement to play Ping-Pong.

When we teach our kids that everyone is exactly who they're meant to be, celebrate the good, and model how to care for one another when we need a little extra support, they're able and willing to step up and help, too. Molly noticed her anxious sister getting overwhelmed and did what she knew I'd do in the same situation in a compassionate, nonjudgmental way.

We can cultivate this supportive atmosphere in our homes by showing compassion always. Show compassion to each other, but also to yourself. Parents, you are your kiddos' only true example of what a happy, healthy parenthood looks like. Sure, they see how their friends' parents behave and treat one another and their kids, but the truth is that everyone behaves with a filter on when they're around people outside their home or when guests are over. You are the only unfiltered view they have of adulthood, so remember to treat yourself the way you want your children to treat themselves when they're adults. Start or renew a hobby, read books, take walks, go for hikes, travel, and show love to yourself and to your family.

Be open with one another about your needs. When my kids were younger, sometimes I'd put a movie on in the afternoon and give them a snack, saying I needed a few minutes of quiet time. I'd go to the gazebo in the back yard and rock on the glider while they watched their movie. Now, my sixteen-year-old does the same. If she's had a lot of people time, she'll head out back to the hammock and swing for a while. My fourteen-year-old will retreat to her room to draw when she needs quiet time. The boys, however, don't seem to ever get enough people time. They're the most extroverted extroverts I've met. As a family, we try to balance the needs of the extroverts and the introverts as best we can. Open communication helps.

One way to keep the communication open is to hold family meetings. These could be weekly or monthly, or even just from time to time, as needed. The goal is to share things that are going well, things the family needs to work on together, and what's coming up so everyone is on the same page. Lorie's family does this well. She and her family go out to a favorite coffee shop every Sunday after church. They have coffee, hot cocoa, scones, or muffins, and compare the weekly calendars so everyone knows what everyone else has coming up over the next few days so they can be there for one another.

Supporting one another means knowing that everyone has different needs, and they're all valid. It means loving each other for exactly who they are. It means being on the same page and recognizing that the family is a better team because of the differences we all bring to the table, and that everyone has something to contribute.

Nurturing Through Shared Experiences

Like James's dad did, find ways to connect with your kids through experiences. Find little ways to have fun with each other. You don't have to do anything elaborate because kids don't need that. Simple goes a long way. Try adding in whole-family rituals, too. Every year for the kids' birthdays, we start the day with "cinnamon roll donut hole cake" for breakfast. This cake is just a cheater version of monkey bread I threw together when Trevor was three by cutting up refrigerator biscuits, rolling the raw dough in cinnamon and sugar, baking it, then drizzling it with icing made from powdered sugar and milk. Trevor thought it was a pile of donut holes with cinnamon roll icing, and the name stuck. He asked me to make it for his birthday every

year, and then on his sisters' birthdays once they came along. By the time
Isaac was born (he's ten years younger than Trevor), the ritual had stuck.

The Best Thing. . .

I like being homeschooled because I don't get
in trouble or yelled at. There are also no tough
spelling tests. We don't have to wait all day for
things either. I don't have to rush when I read
at home. We can go outside whenever we want.

—Ashley, 7

My husband is a terrible cook. For the first dinner he cooked me in
his apartment when we were dating, he boiled canned potatoes – in their
can juice! – added a little butter, baked chicken breasts with no seasoning,
and microwaved a bag of frozen peas. The meal was barely palatable, and
we made a deal early on in our marriage that I would do the cooking and
he would do the dishes. It's served us pretty well, but is a little problematic
when I have to be away for a speaking event. To solve this, my husband
came up with two ideas the kids look forward to.

One is "meatball fondue" night. He bakes an entire bag of frozen meatballs, pulls out anything vaguely resembling a dip from the refrigerator and
places smalls cups of the condiments around the table, puts the piping hot
meatballs on a platter in the center of the table and gives each kid a fork.
They stab the meatballs, choose their dip and eat until they're full. The only
rule is no double dipping. While this sounds absolutely revolting to me, and
I cringe at the idea there's no balance to the meal, the kids love it and it's a
fun thing to do with Dad while Mom is away.

Dad also came up with the Family Taste Test Night. When he knows
I'll be out of town, he picks up a variety of flavors of one type of food. For
example, he once bought fourteen different types of Pringles® potato chips
and put them away until I left for a speaking event. On the night of the taste
test, he numbered each package, set out numbered paper plates with the
corresponding chips on them, taped a large piece of paper to the wall, and
called the kids into the kitchen. They went through each chip flavor one by
one in a blind taste test, ranking their assessments of each on a scale of one
to five. Once they got through each flavor, Dad worked with the kids to
calculate the most popular and least popular flavors.

Activities like this give your kids a shared culture and experiences that will follow them through life. Remember that if life goes in the way it's supposed to, your kids will have each other long after you're gone. These are the kinds of stories that they'll tell around the table on holidays and will pass along to their kids. My husband's family tells the same stories about the aunts and uncles and moms and dads every holiday we get together. They're the same shared experiences they've talked about dozens of times over the years, but nonetheless they laugh until their tears stream.

Shared experiences, no matter how minor, give our relationships a sense of connection and present chances to deepen mutual trust and intimacy. The opportunity to strengthen the meaning of a relationship and deepen our understanding of one another can arise from something as simple as sharing a cup of tea. This can lead to more lasting ties and a greater sense of connection with those around us.

One of the greatest advantages to homeschooling is that it's more than just an alternative to traditional education; it's a lifestyle choice that allows us to play a pivotal role in our kiddos' learning journey. One of the many benefits of homeschooling is the opportunity to create and share meaningful experiences as a family. These shared experiences can have a profound impact on strengthening family relationships, fostering lifelong bonds, and enriching our children's education.

The Best Thing. . .

I like being able to spend time together
as a family.

—Raya, 15

Homeschooling provides the perfect backdrop for exploring educational topics in the real world. Instead of confining learning to a classroom, we can take our kids on field trips, visit museums, go on nature walks, or go to cultural events. These shared experiences allow our families to discover new interests and passions together. Over the last several years, I've made a point to take at least one of my children with me to every speaking event I had. We didn't always have a lot of time outside of the work to play and explore new cities, but we always enjoy the time traveling to the venue, dinners out together, and meeting new people. I know our relationships are strong because of the time we spent together traveling – something we wouldn't have been able to do if they'd been enrolled in a traditional school. Whether it's a trip to a science museum, a visit to a local farm, or an exploration of a historical site, these experiences can make learning a dynamic and memorable journey.

Shared experiences foster open communication within the family. Through these adventures, we create opportunities for our kiddos to ask questions, express their thoughts, and engage in meaningful discussions. These conversations can happen naturally as we explore a museum, hike through a national park, or attend a community event. They not only deepen our child's understanding, but also nurture our family relationships by reinforcing the idea that learning is a lifelong adventure.

When we share meaningful activities, we invite collaboration, whether it's working together to solve a problem on a road trip, preparing a meal as a family, or creating a group project related to a shared interest. These collaborative efforts teach valuable life skills, including teamwork, negotiation, and compromise. They also help family members to appreciate each other's strengths and contributions.

Shared experiences become cherished memories that shape our family's narrative. These experiences often stand out as some of the most significant moments in our children's education and upbringing. Whether it's a summer road trip, a family camping adventure, or even a special project, these shared moments become the building blocks of our family's story. The relationships forged in this way are strong. These memories provide a common ground, a foundation on which our family can grow and thrive. Whether our kiddo is still young or is a teenager on the brink of adulthood, shared experiences remain one of the most powerful things we can cultivate in our homeschools.

Homeschooling isn't just about academics; it's an opportunity to nurture strong family relationships and create lifelong memories. The shared experiences we create with our kids weave the threads of love, understanding, and unity that will make our family strong for life. When we embrace these adventures, we find that they are the glue that keeps our family together, making our homeschooling journey an enriching and unforgettable adventure.

Try This!

- **Understand your child's individual needs:** Recognize that one child might need physical touch for comfort, while another prefers solitude or conversation during challenging moments.
- **Support one another:** Create an environment where family members support each other, including those with neurodivergent needs.
- **Celebrate each family member's strengths:** Recognize the distinct strengths and weaknesses of each child and encourage them to appreciate one another.
- **Lean into whom your child is:** Accept your child's personality and unique needs instead of trying to impose norms.
- **Open communication about needs:** Encourage open communication about each family member's needs.
- **Embrace differences and unique needs:** Understand and honor each family member's unique needs, whether they are extroverted or introverted.
- **Nurturing through shared experiences:** Find opportunities to create shared experiences and bond as a family. Implement ideas like "Meatball Fondue Night" and "Family Taste Test Night" and other unique traditions.

- **Foster open communication:** During family outings, promote discussions, ask questions, and engage in meaningful conversations to deepen mutual understanding.
- **Family's lifelong narrative:** These shared experiences become the building blocks of your family's story, something to pass down and treasure for generations.
- **Homeschooling beyond academics:** Homeschooling provides opportunities to nurture strong family relationships and create lifelong memories through shared experiences.

10 | The Most Important Thing

The most important things in life are the connections you make with others.

—Tom Ford

When they've finished reading, Olivia's mother gives her a kiss and says, "You know, you really wear me out. But I love you anyway." And Olivia kisses her back and says, "I love you anyway too."

—From *Olivia* by Ian Falconer

Kara and her family were at the lowest that they had been when she and I met at a homeschool conference for families homeschooling kids who were gifted or had special needs. They had just gone through several family crises that brought a lot of stress into their home. They'd always homeschooled in an outside-the-box way, as their oldest kiddo, Andy, was wired differently, and they knew he would not do well in a regular school environment.

As the stress built, Kara had defaulted to a more traditional method of schooling. Often, when we're under stress, we default to our old ways of doing things, right? It feels like too much work to stay creative, and it's so much easier to pull out a workbook or make kids sit and do busywork. You know it's not the best method for them, but you're just too tired to do anything else. Kara, Andy, and their family were in survival mode and couldn't find their way out.

She recalls the light going out of Andy's eyes, and the constant state of antagonistic refusal he lived in any time she brought out anything that looked remotely academic. This kiddo had always been insatiably curious, full of energy, and bursting with life. She wasn't sure what she hoped to get out of a home-school conference at that point, but she knew she needed help and remembers slipping into one of my sessions, not knowing what to expect. She says:

> I don't even remember how old [Andy] was, but I vividly remember sitting in your workshop and just crying. I felt like somebody finally understood my kid. Somebody understood the challenges that we were facing. I wasn't alone. But then you helped me see what was beneath the surface and what this kid was all about. Who he was and what these challenges might be masking. You helped me remember so much of what was good in there, and that limitless potential that he had. And how amazingly and differently he thought about things.

The Best Thing. . .

I love to play on the trampoline while I do
math practice.

—Isabella, 6

Kara realized that there was no wonder he was having a hard time. He was being asked to do things in a way that he wasn't designed to do them. "He is wired in a way that makes it difficult for him to handle the stress that we were going through. That conference took the pressure off of how things were and helped me to step back and just focus on rebuilding the connection I once had with him." She went on to say, "I just kind of let go of so many of the expectations I had been placing on him and just focused on our relation-ship. I turned my attention to building up an emotional connection so he felt secure. And I really took time for us to get to know each other again." The light came back into his eyes and the shift changed everything for them. Kara said it changed the trajectory of where they were headed.

Kara started to see Andy for who he was; not for the challenges he showed. Kara learned that stressed and scared kids will show you their worst, while safe and loved kids will show you their best. She was determined, at that point, to create an atmosphere in their home that was built on love and connection and emotional safety, and that change has allowed him to bring his best self forward again. She ends by saying, "Turning our focus on connecting with Andy and building our relationship first as you said in that talk changed our lives. You helped me fall in love with my son again."

Connection, Connection, Connection

Connection means everything when it comes to helping our kids relate to the world and boost their learning. And our kids need it more than they ever have before. As Dr. Daniel Franklin says in his book *Helping Your Child with Language-Based Learning Disabilities*, "The most crucial factor for successful education, is not what you'd expect. It's not the curriculum or the textbooks; it's the dynamic relationship between the learner and their teacher." Adam Grant, psychologist and author of the book *Hidden Potential: The Science of Achieving Greater Things*, agrees and takes it further. In his book he writes, "Finland and Estonia have world-class schools. One of their secrets is looping: teachers move up with their students. Data from approximately three million kids shows that it works in the United States too. Students learn more when they happen to have the same teacher again. Extended relationships unlock hidden potential." Homeschooling is the ultimate looping situation. Not only do our kids have the same teacher for their entire schooling experience, but that teacher is the one who loves them the most, advocates for them the hardest, and will move any mountain to find a way to give them exactly what they need to be successful.

For many of us, the reason we chose to homeschool in the first place was because we knew that connection mattered, and we wanted the opportunity to really connect and engage with our kids. It's not just about putting in the time, though. We need to be deliberate and purposeful and we build those connections. This becomes even more critical when we're parenting children who have unique needs, especially those with social-emotional challenges that might affect the typical parent-child connection. Connection serves as the cornerstone for everything else — learning, social and emotional skills, how our kids navigate the world, their resilience, and even dealing with anxiety. When that strong parent-child connection is the bedrock, all these aspects become much more manageable.

Research consistently supports the importance of connection in all areas of our kids' lives, starting in our homes. Kids need to feel that they're safe and secure with their family. They should have confidence that their physical, social, emotional, mental, and academic needs will be met. It's all about laying a strong foundation at home, but it doesn't stop there. Connection plays a huge role in every aspect of our lives. It's not confined to our homes; it spreads to our extended family, friends, neighbors, and the larger community. When our kids have a stable foundation and healthy relationships within the family, they can confidently go out and make a positive impact on the world. For instance, my eleven-year-old and I decided to whip up some treats and deliver them to relatives dealing with illness. It's a small gesture, but it's all about creating those human connections.

The Best Thing. . .

Our relationship got better when my parents
started homeschooling me, and my family became
my best friends. This meant that we could talk
about important things without getting angry.
I am thankful that they taught me how to be wise
and discerning.

—Hunter, 16

Active Engagement

In my experience, establishing a strong connection with my kids at home always begins with me actively engaging in their world and interests. Now, I understand that some might be thinking, *I'd love to connect with my kids, but the daily grind is tough.* Where they are is precisely where I would recommend starting. It's about taking a closer look at what piques their interest, whether it's a video game, or in my case, my youngest's newfound passion for making board games. For me, it meant playing each new game he created with him, offering feedback as requested, even if I had other things to do. I took on the role of the supportive sounding board, offering suggestions for improvement and helping him find the inconsistencies in his rules. It's about embracing what matters to them, no matter how trivial it might seem, and that's a fantastic starting point for building those connections.

Shawna's oldest son was very interested in saltwater aquariums for many years so the two of them spent a great deal of time visiting aquarium stores and talking with experts. It may sound frivolous on the surface but spending the time to take him to a place where he could dream, ask questions, and learn about a passion meant the world to him. He's now in college and their relationship is still strong.

Even if it sometimes feels a bit draining to spend an hour strolling around an aquarium store or being the mom sitting in the back of the theater, watching your child learn new choreography again and again, the benefits are truly substantial. They far outweigh the idea of insisting on some kind of formal journal entry to document their interest in fish or game creation. The value of these moments far outshines making them do a chore or workbook page instead of letting them dive into what they're most passionate about. It's not that those chores and responsibilities aren't essential, but I've found it's often better to lean toward nurturing what my child is genuinely passionate about. After all, that's who they are meant to be.

I genuinely want to honor and appreciate the value these interests bring to our home, and it pays off by strengthening our connections. In our homeschool, this often translates into me sitting beside them while they're engrossed in video games, attempting to grasp their enthusiasm, and having them showcase their impressive feats in Minecraft. They might proudly declare, "Look, I conquered this particular setting," or something along those lines. I'm not much of a gamer myself, and I confess I don't understand most of the games they play. However, I make it a point to stay informed about what they're playing, acting as their biggest cheerleader and someone genuinely interested in embracing their interests. This simple effort significantly bolsters our connection, and it seamlessly extends into all the aspects of our homeschool.

The Best Thing. . .

It was hard to stay out of trouble when I went to school. I wanted to be accepted, but the "cool kids" had rules to join their group. They would say things like, "You can't be our friend unless you...." I stole a Barbie doll from the grocery store to fit in with this group. I had to tearfully give it back when my parents found the doll. This made them decide to homeschool me. I loved it. There was no pressure to be someone I wasn't anymore. No peer pressure at all. The atmosphere was much more relaxed, and I loved my new group of friends—my family and homeschooling friends. Homeschooling gave me a fresh start and healthy relationships with good people, and drew me closer to my family.

—Jess, 17

It comes down to knowing your child well. When you do, you'll know how to help that connection along, whether it's between the two of you or with a sibling or friend. I mentioned Logan's empathy earlier in this book. She's always thinking about other people and seeks to connect with her friends and siblings by coming up with fun things to add to their lives. One thing she does is create little scavenger hunts for her siblings. The two older kids roll their eyes because she spends all day writing, then wants them to stop what they're doing to go on her hunt. While her clues are getting more and more clever, the other kids don't always want to stop what they're doing, but it always makes them feel loved when they do.

I try to encourage them all to participate, and give Logan little prizes to hide at the end of her scavenger hunts. Once I explained to the older kids that taking a few minutes out of their free time to solve their sister's clues and find the candy I give her to hide at the end fills her emotional bucket, as Tom Rath and Mary Reckmeyer wrote about in *How Full Is Your Bucket for Kids*, a book I read with all my kids, they were more willing to join in. It goes back to having set up a culture within our home that we're a team and need to support one another. The candy doesn't hurt either.

Connecting with Older Kids

It's not always easy to connect once they're older, but it's still important to try. My sixteen-year-old loves getting various members of her family to try out silly social media dances. I am a terrible dancer, and everyone knows it. But I still try, and often make myself seem even worse so she has something to laugh about. Sometimes we think, as parents, *I don't like this*, or *I don't like that*. When it comes to connecting with our kids, the point is to think about what they like. I already mentioned that I don't like video games. I'm not opposed to them, but there are things I'd much rather be doing. But it's my job as a parent to meet them where they are, so I'll try playing from time to time.

For one of my kids, her "love language" is gifts. She adores giving and receiving them. Whenever I can, I pick up a pack of gum, or a sticker, or a treat she particularly likes and give it to her. It makes her feel loved and know I was thinking about her while I was away. That strengthens our connection and usually leads to long talks or a hug. Think outside the box and know that little, teeny, tiny things go a long way with our kids. I heard Sally Clarkson, author of *Different: The Story of an Outside-the-Box Kid and the Mom Who Loved Him*, say at a conference once: teenagers connect with you at the worst possible time. It's usually when it's late, and after you've been together all day long. Our teens find us around 11:00 p.m., we're exhausted and ready for bed, and they talk until 1:00 a.m., pouring out their hearts and souls to us. Connecting in those moments is powerful. Tiring, but so important to them.

I don't want anyone reading this to think that connection has to somehow rule your life and homeschool or be like another thing on your to-do list. Don't stress out and think, *well now I must figure out all these ways to connect with my kids all day long.* The reality is they're your children, and you know them best. This is about intentionality. It's about us taking the time to find little ways that make the biggest difference in our relationships, then going with them. Most importantly, it's about us enjoying them in the process.

A Soft Place to Land

I overheard a conversation in a coffee shop while I was working the other day and can't get it out of my mind. Two older moms had met for lunch and were talking about a third who had canceled on them at the last minute. It seems this missing friend needed to drive two hours to the town her twenty-something son had been living in to help him move back home. They didn't have all the details, but they knew their friend's son had broken up with the woman he'd dated and moved for, and was moving home for a while. They didn't hide their thoughts on this development. "If my son called me and wanted to move back home because he'd broken up with his girlfriend, I'd remind him that he's an adult and needs to suck up life's disappointments." The other agreed and added, "I told my daughter that she could come back home on college breaks, but once she graduated, she was on her own."

The Best Thing. . .

We can choose our own curriculum and I'm not forced into anything. I'm always involved in the big decisions.

—Lincoln, 12

Inside my head, I applauded the missing friend. Parenting doesn't end once our kids hit young adulthood, and I want my kids to know I'm there for them *always*. My cousin Nancy is one of the best examples of motherhood I have, and for years, I've held her up as the person I most want to be like. Her three children are grown: one is married with the sweetest toddler ever to be born and a darling husband who dotes on his little family; and the other two have graduated college and are making their way in the world. I've watched as her grown kids tag her in recipes they know she'll like on Facebook, share social media posts about her taking her grandson to pumpkin patches or for sleepovers, and how they come home when jobs change, relationships falter, or celebrations are to be had. They have their lives, so they're not there constantly, but it's clear they know that the door is always open at home.

I want to be that mom. When my adult kids feel overwhelmed or need a place to retreat to and cry, I want them to know they always have the option to come home to family. We will always welcome them with open arms. We won't criticize them for choosing to run away from their problems to take time to get back on their feet. We won't question them about what is going on; instead, we'll wait until they're ready to talk. We will just open the front door, give our adult kids a hug, and direct them to the pantry, where they'll find their favorite snacks and drinks.

Some people, like the women in the café, may be under the impression that it is immature of an adult child to want seek refuge in the house where they grew up. They feel that kids need to grow tough, push through tough times, be an adult, and figure it out on their own. I'm grateful I have a model like Nancy because I can begin now and send the message to my kids that I love them without conditions and will always be here for them. Nan's relationship with her kids is the kind of relationship I hope to have with my children when they reach adulthood and become independent.

Knowing that there is a place they can go where they'll always be loved will give our kids an incredible sense of security. They're free to make errors, pursue their dreams, and even fall flat on their faces when they know there are people who love them and there's a cozy home they can come back to and heal from mistakes.

The Best Thing. . .

I know I am loved and valued by the people
I am surrounded with and they'll always be
there for me.

—Brody, 12

I first heard the suggestion to be a soft place to land from a psychologist we were working with when Trevor was very young. At the time, we were going down the same path so many parents do and trying to figure out what was wrong with him so we could fix him to help him be successful in school. I'd just left teaching and was freelancing as an educational writer with two other tiny kiddos at home. I was trying to help him be successful at school, and his psychologist told me that the reason he fell apart on me when he got home each afternoon was because I was his soft place to land. Like a crash pad that breaks the fall of a runaway truck, I was Trevor's safe space where he could fall apart after trying desperately to hold it together all day long while he was away.

It was heartbreaking to watch this little guy, once so curious, melt into a puddle at my feet almost as soon as he stepped foot off the school bus. It was also validating for me as a parent that I was doing something so right for him at home that he felt completely safe and secure in his knowledge that I'd never go away. Being his soft place to land and having that psychologist validate our relationship was just one of the catalysts that sent us down the path of homeschooling. But it also transformed my parenting mindset. Instead of looking for what was wrong, I began to see Trevor, and then my other kids, as the whole people they are and realized that I didn't want to *fix* anything about them. I wanted them to know their values are in them, not a result of anything they do or don't do. I wanted to be their soft place to land, now, when they're young, and long into their adult lives just like my cousin Nan is for her kids.

Being Their Person

It was another late night for me, and I knew I'd be exhausted in the morning when my youngest stomped his way down the stairs from his bedroom to the kitchen. The stairs go right above my bed, so he stomps to make sure I know he's up, as youngest children who crave attention are wont to do. I had another hour of work to do, though, and had lost the original time I'd set aside to do it as my teen needed to talk.

Parenting is filled with joys and challenges. One of the most rewarding aspects is being your child's person, the one whom they turn to for guidance, love, and support. Being my daughter's person is a role I'd never give up, despite the lack of sleep, because I know it's precious. I have a strong connection with each of my kids and trust it will have a profound positive impact on their emotional development, self-esteem, and overall well-being.

Being your child's person means being the person they feel most comfortable and safe with. It builds off the idea that your home is their soft place to land and gives them the added security of knowing there's always someone there to listen. It's about creating a deep emotional connection with your child, so they trust you with their thoughts, feelings, and problems. It's a role that extends beyond the traditional duties of parenting and taps into the emotional foundation of the parent-child relationship.

From tots to teens, our kiddos will go through a wide range of emotions as they grow and navigate life. When we can be our child's person, we give them a sounding board to express their feelings and concerns without judgment. This emotional support helps them develop healthy ways of dealing with their emotions and promotes resilience. Sometimes that sounding board ends up being more of a wailing wall or a verbal punching bag, but when they have a safe person in us, they can grow and develop outside our homes with more success.

My oldest daughter started doing theater productions with a local all-boys Catholic preparatory school in the area over the last few years, along with several teen-only shows at various local community theaters, and after one rehearsal, she said to me that she was surprised at how many of the kids she's met don't talk to or trust their parents. She chatted about a particular conversation she and a few of the kids had about journals and diaries over the break at rehearsal that night. She told me that the consensus was that if you kept a journal it needed to be hidden well or locked up because their parents would read it if they found it. She asked if that was really a thing, "Do parents actually search kids' rooms and read through their journals? It never occurred to me that someone, especially a parent, would do that. Would you?"

I told her that no, I wouldn't search her room and read anything of hers without permission, with one exception. I told her that if I ever thought she was in danger, making unsafe choices, or was a threat to herself I'd go through every drawer and read every scrap of paper I could find to help her. She looked at me, shrugged, then said, "Well I would hope that you'd violate my trust if I were in crisis. How else is someone going to get the help they need when they need it most if the person closest to them doesn't find a way to offer it?" Trust is crucial in a parent–child relationship, especially when we want our kiddos to be able to come to us. My kids know that they can trust me in whatever areas they need support. I won't violate their trust unless they or someone else is in danger.

This level of trust encourages open communication. It allows our children to feel comfortable discussing their thoughts, experiences, and problems with us. This open dialogue is crucial for understanding our kids' perspective and helping them make informed decisions. Paradoxically, being our child's person encourages independence. When our children feel secure in our support, they are more likely to explore the world, make choices, take healthy risks, and learn from their mistakes, knowing that we are there to guide them.

The Best Thing. . .

I loved homeschooling because I never feel different, broken, or wrong. My homeschooling friends played with me as they might play with anyone else, and my parents helped me see that my differences weren't flaws, they were what make me unique.

—Maya, 13

So, for now, and probably for the next decade as my youngest is still only ten years old, I'll be setting up to work in my office once the home-school day, evening activities, and bedtime routines have wrapped up, only to be interrupted by a kiddo looking to spend a little time talking to their person and finding their soft place to land.

Try This!

- **Prioritize connection:** Set aside dedicated family time without distractions, like no screens or cellphones during dinner.
- **Dynamic relationships:** Foster open communication with your child. Ask about their day, interests, and challenges regularly.
- **Be deliberate and purposeful:** Plan special activities with your child, like art projects, cooking together, or nature walks.
- **Strong parent-child connection:** Use bedtime routines to have meaningful conversations and express your love and support.
- **Safe and secure home:** Create a loving and stable home environment where your child knows they can always turn to you for help and comfort.
- **Extend connection:** Encourage your child to maintain connections with extended family members through regular visits, phone calls, or video chats.
- **Acts of kindness:** Engage in acts of kindness together, like baking cookies for a neighbor or making cards for friends.

- **Quality time:** Plan outings related to your child's interests, such as visiting a museum if they love art or a nature reserve if they enjoy wildlife.
- **Support sibling connections:** Encourage siblings to work on projects together, play games, or collaborate on family activities.
- **Connect with teens:** Engage with your teenager's hobbies, even if you're not naturally inclined. Attend their events and show interest in their friends.
- **Love languages:** Discover your child's love language and surprise them with small gestures like their favorite snacks or a heartfelt note.
- **Late-night conversations:** Be available for late-night talks with your teenagers, and actively listen to their concerns without judgment.
- **Be Intentional, not overwhelming:** Find meaningful moments for connection, such as a shared morning routine or a daily family dinner.
- **A soft place to land:** Ensure your home is a welcoming and non-judgmental place where your adult children can always find support and comfort.

11 | Start Now

We can sum up very quickly what people need to teach their own children. First of all, they have to like them, enjoy their company, their physical presence, their energy, foolishness, and passion. They have to enjoy all their talk and questions, and enjoy equally trying to answer those questions. They have to think of their children as friends, indeed very close friends, have to feel happier when they are near and miss them when they are away. They have to trust them as people, respect their fragile dignity, treat them with courtesy, take them seriously. They have to feel in their own hearts some of their children's wonder, curiosity, and excitement about the world. And they have to have enough confidence in themselves, skepticism about experts, and willingness to be different from most people, to take on themselves the responsibility for their children's learning. But that is about all that parents need.

—John Holt

But then I realized, what do they really know? This is MY idea, I thought. No one knows it like I do. And it's okay if it's different, and weird, and maybe a little crazy.
—From *What Do You Do with an Idea?* by Kobi Yamada

It was the Tuesday before Thanksgiving, and Trevor hung his head as he stepped off the school bus. I'd expected him to bound down those stairs with excitement and energy; after all, he was heading into a five-day weekend that included Thanksgiving, his birthday, and my birthday. It would be full of celebrations and fun. I slipped his backpack onto my own shoulder, put my arm around him, and asked what happened. He looked up at me then, my sweet little boy, the once extreme thinker eager for school to come so he could "learn more and more and more," with eyes swimming. "If I can't have an all-green week on a two-day week," he said, "I'll never earn Tiger Cash." My biggest parenting regret is that I didn't pull him from school right then and start homeschooling immediately.

You see, we'd talked a little about homeschooling. He's the one who brought it up initially. He'd read a book that had a homeschool family in it and he'd seen TV shows that featured homeschooling families, too. I was scared, though. I didn't know anyone else who homeschooled their kids, and I'd been a teacher and educational consultant for more than a decade. My husband was a teacher. It's all we knew. That Tuesday I promised him I'd learn what I could about homeschooling and see if it would be a good fit for our family. Then I encouraged him to put it out of his mind so he could enjoy the holiday and birthday weekend.

Over the next few weeks, I researched all I could about homeschooling. I think back on that time, and think it was both easier and more difficult to get information about something like homeschooling. It was 2010, and I did Google searches, landed on blogs, and checked out books from the library. There were no Facebook groups divided by state, county, and city. Instagram had just launched the month before that little boy walked off the bus with tears in his eyes. Podcasts, while they'd been around for a while, wouldn't gain popularity for another four or five years. And TikTok wouldn't exist for six more years. Most bloggers and books suggested new homeschoolers hang out in the kids' section of the library or at parks during the school day to find other homeschoolers in their area.

It was so much harder to get started when you didn't know other homeschoolers because resources and groups weren't a click away, and there weren't as many as there are now. It was easier for the same reason. It took me until February to build up the courage to pull Trevor out of school. I'd been gathering information, curriculum, and planning since Thanksgiving, but was nervous. My husband and I went in for his early February parent-teacher conference, told his teacher he wouldn't be back, and cleaned out his desk.

The Best Thing. . .

At home, I didn't need to go with the flow
of 20-some other kids. I could work at my
own pace. I struggled with ADHD, executive
functioning difficulties, and sensory processing
disorder. Sitting in a classroom and focusing on an
assignment was next to impossible for me. There
were so many distractions, and it didn't matter if
the work was too easy or too hard; getting it done
in the timeframe needed was tough.

—Trevor, 21

Looking back, I should not have sent him back to school after Thanksgiving that year. His classroom was not a good fit for him, and neither was the teacher he had that year. It took a long time for us to work through social, emotional, mental, and even some academic damage that was done. I wish I'd had someone there to tell me that I should pull him out and that I could do "this homeschool thing" because maybe I'd have had the courage I needed sooner than I did. So, I'm here to tell you . . .

You've Got This!

For the past several years, I have traveled the United States and Canada to speak to families at homeschool conferences and conventions. Many of them were attending to learn more about homeschooling to prepare for pulling their kids out of a traditional, and often negative, school setting. Some had small children and knew they wanted to keep them home once they were school-aged. Others were homeschool veterans and were there for some inspiration for the coming year.

I said the same thing to all of them when they wondered if they could or should homeschool. I want to tell you the same thing – *You are the absolute best parent and teacher for your child. You know them better than anyone. You can do this, and anytime you doubt, just let me know. Find me on social media or email through my website and let me know you're doubting. I'll point you to resources that will help or just give you a pep talk.*

I'm not the only one who'd do this for you, either. I asked longtime readers, podcast listeners, followers, and homeschool friends what they'd say to someone who doubted they could do it or was nervous about getting started. The results were overwhelmingly encouraging. The biggest recurring message, though, was ***just start***! "Stop overthinking," Janice said, "and just do it. Just like parenting itself, you'll make mistakes, learn from them, and change what you're doing. If you start now, you can get going on those mistakes so you can fix them sooner." I'd add that a bad day homeschooling with the people you love will always be better than the best day in a setting that doesn't fit your child or hurts their social, emotional, or mental well-being.

Know the Laws

Even though homeschooling is more mainstream than it was even fifteen years ago when I started, parents are often worried about the legality of it. The best advice I can give is to research the laws in the state or country you're in and follow them completely. If you're in the United States, know that homeschooling is legal in all fifty states, though the regulations vary depending on the state in which you live. Some states are heavily regulated and require you to fill out paperwork or notify that you're homeschooling. Some have little to no oversight at all. It's important for you to do your own

research on this and know the laws specific to you so you can follow them. You can find links to help you with this research at www.homeschool advantage.resources. Remember, though, you're not replicating school at home; you're homeschooling. The goal is to learn the laws so you can work within their framework to make homeschooling your own.

Know Your Why

Jennie says, "The only expert on your child is you. Trust yourself and have fun in the process." Most people go into homeschooling for a reason. My family started homeschooling because our son's needs were not being met, and he was starting to feel like a failure. Worse, he was convinced he was a bad person. Kendra's situation was similar, and she agrees that it's important to start sooner rather than later if you're thinking about homeschooling: "The No Child Left Behind Act has left so many children behind. You can do more for your child at home than the system ever could. You love your child best, therefore you'll fight to give him everything he needs socially, emotionally, and academically." And so many current and former educators agree that the one-on-one nature of homeschooling gives kids an advantage no traditional schooling model can replicate.

We started homeschooling because we knew that we could meet our son's individualized needs better than a teacher with a classroom full of varying needs could. And like Elise told me when I asked what she'd say to a nervous new homeschooler, "You will never regret the time you spend with your children, and homeschooling gives you more of it." And like Kriste who says, "You can always change your mind and put them back in school," we decided to take a year-by-year and kid-by-kid approach to homeschooling our children. Fifteen years later, we're still homeschooling and have graduated one of them. Kriste went on to advise parents of young kids, "If you're worrying about high school, don't. You can figure it out as you go."

Carly agrees, "It's okay to go slow and figure things out along the way." She advises parents, "love your child more than your checklist." No matter what finally brought us to choose homeschooling, it's probable kids were at the center of our decision, whether they'd been having trouble in school, were advanced and we wanted to be able to allow them to keep accelerating, or we have specific moral, spiritual, or pedagogical reasons, the center is always our kiddos. Becca reminds us of that center and says, "Focus on the joy of getting to know your kids, their interests, and what can bring their spark back. Learning will follow with a strong foundation of joy."

Know Your Kids

Over the years, we've had smooth seasons of homeschooling, and we've had rough ones. Almost every time we've struggled has been because I've let myself fall back on my public-school training and instituted strict schedules, formal lessons of my choosing, and have separated concepts out into distinct subjects. I know my kids well, and they learn so much better when they are learning things in the context of real-life and multiple subjects are integrated together. You know your kids well, too. When we remember who our kids are and how they learn best, homeschooling becomes a lifestyle, not another thing to add to the plate. This is just one more reason to start now. Sarah reminds us, "You WILL figure it out, as a family, one step at a time." We just need to allow ourselves to get started. Do not make the mistake of overgeneralizing and giving up when things don't go as planned. Instead, observe, take a break, and try something else. You will find the rhythm that fits you best. Transitions take time, so give yourself a break.

The Best Thing. . .

I can sleep in or choose to get up and get an early start on my schoolwork. I love that we can make our own schedule. There was a period of time when I would get up, grab a granola bar, and get my independent work done before 11:00 am each day. Not anymore, unfortunately, but I'm working on reregulating my daily rhythm. For now, I often stay up late watching a movie with my older brother because I know he'll be moving out soon, and I then sleep in a bit. I love that I have the flexibility to have that choice.

—Molly, 16

The Need to Deschool

We're accidental homeschoolers, forged in the fires of failed public school attempts, and absolutely thriving now. It has taken time and trials to get us into the rhythm we have now – lots of time and lots of trials. Over the years, we've been able to fine-tune each kiddo's education for their specific needs in a way the schools were just unable to. We are in the homeschooling zone now, and have even successfully graduated one with another soon to follow. First, though, we had to deschool.

Deschooling is one of those words we spot often enough in homeschooling groups that we know it's real, but we're not always sure what exactly it is. *Deschooling* is, in its simplest terms, recovering from public school. It's like hitting the reset button so our kiddos can regroup and learn to learn again. It serves many purposes, both for the homeschooling parent and the child, but the main idea is that when we choose to remove our children from traditional schooling environments and bring them home, there's a period of adjustment and healing that must take place before we can truly spread our wings as homeschoolers.

In a traditional school setting, kids are taught to be good students. They typically learn to patiently wait for a teacher to dictate what they should do, learn, and think. Curiosity can take a back seat, and our kiddos can focus on facts and figures, not the playfulness of imagination. Deschooling is like hitting a reset button and letting our kids learn to love learning again. Christy-Faith, author of *Homeschool Rising: Shattering Myths, Finding Courage, and Opting Out of the School System*, said, "I feel like what we're really doing is reclaiming childhoods with the homeschool movement," on a recent episode of The Homeschool Conversations Podcast.

And reclaim childhood we should. Homeschooling is all about allowing a child to rediscover that natural love for learning that they were born with but has been dulled by the rigidity of traditional education. Taking some time to deschool gives our kiddos a chance to set their curiosity free and nurture their interests again. When our kiddos are homeschooled, they have the gift of time — time to explore ideas that genuinely intrigue and matter to them. And this is when authentic, profound learning takes place.

Deschooling isn't a vacation or a free-for-all. It's not a time to lounge in your pajamas and play video games all day, though we can do some of that from time to time. Deschooling isn't a break from learning; it's a pause from what we've always done as we ease into what we're about to do. It's an important process for new homeschooling parents to go through. If you find yourself unexpectedly homeschooling, there will be an adjustment period, and you will be bombarding yourself with resources, methods, curriculum choices, and more. You'll find yourself suddenly responsible for a lot more than you ever expected, and if you're not careful, you can get swept away. Deschooling gives homeschoolers a chance to find our footing.

It gives us permission to let go of how we've always thought learning had to be and explore new, unexpected, and outside-the-box ways of learning. When all we've known of education has been a desk in a classroom and we find ourselves seated at the kitchen table with an expectant child, the temptation is great to try and re-create the school experience at home. It's important to note that even if a parent comes into homeschooling from the beginning, there's still a time of reframing what learning is because the traditional model of education is likely all that parent knows.

In Trevor's case, public school had begun to cause him trauma. As a neurodivergent kiddo, an extreme thinker, and asynchronous learner, the last thing he needed was to reproduce the same environment and the same ways of learning. He needed the freedom to explore, to follow his interests, to discover all the different ways he could learn from all the different resources that exist beyond textbooks. He needed a break, he needed permission to be himself. That's the gift deschooling offers. So often, new homeschoolers struggle. We withdraw our kiddos on a Friday, and by Monday, our child wakes up to worksheets. We're afraid of educational holes, falling behind, and feel that we have to keep the momentum going. Fear drives us to jump into the homeschooling deep-end. The last thing we want to do is drown ourselves in the first week.

After years of bells and schedules and rows and lines, we all need time to re-set our minds and free ourselves from the idea that learning must begin promptly at 8:00 a.m. and stop by 3:00 p.m. Learning is not like crossing monkey bars, where you must swing into the next level or subject before you lose your forward motion. It's a lifestyle that has ebb and flow, and deschooling allows for this ebb. This doesn't mean spending all day on the couch; it means finding ways to sneak learning in without making it seem like learning. Some of the things we can do as we begin our homeschooling adventures to de-school, sneak some learning in, have fun with our kids, and give us time to acclimate include:

- visiting museums
- watching documentaries
- playing with science kits
- reading books together
- exploring nature
- visiting the library
- creating in Minecraft
- playing board games
- learning new computer programs
- taking apart old electronics
- trying out music lessons
- testing a new art style
- sharing deep conversations

When we share in activities like this, we get a firsthand look at how much learning can take place in nontraditional and informal ways. Instead of fighting to make school-at-home happen, we'll gain the confidence to explore and discover what works best for our families.

The Best Thing. . .

I don't mind doing some things, you need to know them.... I like that I kinda have a say in our decisions so I can know what my future is.
—Lincoln, 12

Deschooling is a great time to learn more about what makes our kiddos tick, what excites them, and to strengthen our connection as we begin a new journey. It's an opportunity to build a foundation before we add a stack of curriculum. But just how long is this honeymoon phase supposed to last?

Well, that depends. Most people agree that we should plan for one month of deschooling for every year our kids have spent in school. It sounds like a lot, especially if we have had our kiddos going to a traditional school for several years, but remember that during this time we're re-programming the way we see education, and our reaction is most likely due to the myth that learning needs to take place five days a week between the months of September and May. We're not bound by a school district's calendar and schedule, and we don't need to waste time on test prep, review, calming rowdy classes, and transition time in the hallways. Our kiddos aren't missing as much as we think.

Trevor took over a year to deschool. He was still learning during this time, but we did no structured curriculum. Erin says her son was begging for a test within two weeks of being pulled from school. He craved the structure of the worksheets and tests he'd been used to, so she balanced the fun, sneaky learning she wanted to help move him toward with the structured classroom-like learning he'd been used to. There is no tried-and-true formula for deschooling, just as there is no one way to homeschool. The important thing is to listen to our children, to respond to their needs, to ease into homeschooling as slowly or quickly as you all need to.

If we are new to homeschooling or are about to embark on the rewarding journey that is home education, we need to do ourselves a favor and leave some room for deschooling. We need it. Our kiddos need it. Our home-schools will be better off for it. We should allow ourselves the time to change our minds about what learning has to look like. Our children have the rest of their lives to learn, but the time to rest and discover is rare and fleeting, so we must take it, protect it, and enjoy it.

Try This!

- **Deschooling:** During the deschooling phase, focus on activities like reading for pleasure, visiting museums, and exploring educational apps without structured lessons.
- **Reclaim childhood:** Encourage your child to engage in creative play, exploration, and self-directed learning activities.
- **Lifestyle learning:** Incorporate learning into everyday life by discussing scientific phenomena during nature walks, cooking together to explore math concepts, or using board games to teach critical thinking.
- **Relax and observe:** If a particular curriculum or approach isn't working, take a step back, identify areas of struggle, and explore alternative methods.
- **Time for deschooling:** Allocate time for deschooling where learning is less structured, focusing on your child's interests.
- **Flexible schedules:** Be open to spontaneous learning opportunities and adjust your daily schedule to accommodate your child's natural learning rhythm.
- **Child-centered approach:** Experiment with project-based learning, field trips, or discussion-based lessons that align with your child's interests.
- **Adjust to individual needs:** Customize your approach for each child, offering different resources, materials, or activities based on their unique requirements.
- **Embrace unconventional learning:** Allow your child to explore their interests through hands-on activities, experiments, and personal projects.
- **Be patient with the process:** Embrace the learning curve, acknowledging that adapting to homeschooling is a journey filled with adjustments.

- **Lifelong learning journey:** Encourage your child to continue learning beyond the traditional school calendar by pursuing their interests during school breaks.
- **Customized learning paths:** Embrace the uniqueness of your homeschooling journey, allowing your child to explore their passions and choose learning pathways that resonate with them.

12 | Final Thoughts

From the day you became a parent, you also became a teacher, and you are equipped to be a teacher.

—Anne Campbell

You're braver than you believe, stronger than you seem, and smarter than you think.

—From *Winnie-the-Pooh* by A.A. Milne

A few weeks after I pulled Trevor out of his first-grade class, I was shopping with him at a nearby Target in the middle of the day. I rounded the corner with my cart, four-year-old Molly sitting in the basket and one-year-old Logan sitting in the child seat, and almost bumped into Marilyn, a kindergarten teacher I had worked with in my previous school district where I'd been a gifted intervention specialist, and the grandmother to a boy in Trevor's first-grade class. She looked surprised to see us shopping in the middle of the school day and stopped to talk.

"Hi there, Trevor!" she addressed him first. "Are you sick today?" He told her he didn't go to school anymore and was homeschooling now. Marilyn was shocked and made no effort to hide her disapproval. At the time, I was still nervous about the decision, and I quickly stammered some reasons – his needs weren't being met, he'd tested gifted and ADHD, but couldn't get services, and we thought, since I was working from home anyway, it'd make sense to homeschool him so I could give him the education he deserved and not have to be up at the school every day fighting for accommodations that would never come.

Marilyn looked at me with what seemed like disgust, and told me I was a disappointment to my profession and students in that district. That with my background in gifted and special needs, I should be keeping him in school, and working toward getting policies changed for all the parents who don't know what I do about gifted and twice-exceptional children. She told me I'd regret it and that children belonged in a school setting because it was the right way to learn. That I was harming my child's future.

The Best Thing. . .

We can make an outing to the grocery store into a learning experience if we want to. But, because the homeschooling community is so incredible in our area, we don't have to. There are always cool things to choose from in the area. Right now I'm taking "Homeschooling with Horses" where we spend two hours each week in the barn, grooming, riding, hitching to carts, testing the DNA of the horses to determine the rescue animals' bloodlines, and so much more. How cool is that?

—Logan, 14

Over the years I've thought about this encounter several times. There are so many things I wish I'd said to Marilyn.

I wish I'd told her that it would have been irresponsible to sacrifice my son's education to advocate for potential change that likely wouldn't come until it was too late to benefit him, if it came at all. I wish I had said that homeschooling is a gift that pays off for a lifetime. That it's a privilege to be home with my kids. That kids are rushed out of their homes and away from their parents too soon, and we need to hold on to them for as long as we can.

I wish I could go back and tell her that homeschooling works. That there are as many ways to homeschool as there are homeschoolers.

Instead, I'll tell you.

Since that run-in at Target, I've spoken to thousands of homeschoolers around the world from the stage at large conventions, at smaller conferences, in breakout sessions, through virtual summits, and one on one. There have been parents who homeschool in just about every way you can think: with boxed curriculums, classically, using the Charlotte Mason method, eclectically, or completely unschool.

Here's the thing – the method of homeschooling doesn't really matter as much as you think it does when you're in the trenches.

Homeschooling works.

You love your kids more than anyone else does. You are their best advocate, teacher, advisor, and confidante. You are the absolute best parent **and** teacher for *your* specific kids because nobody else can love them like you do or know them as well. Whether you follow a very specific boxed curriculum, subscribe to a known methodology, or piece it together as you go, vacillating between resources, *homeschooling works*.

It works because you get to make it *yours*.

It works because you care; there is nobody better suited for this job than you.

The Best Thing. . .

My favorite part of homeschooling is the relationship I have with my brother and sisters. I'm ten
years younger than my big brother, but he's still
my best friend.

—Isaac, 10

You aren't tied to one way of doing things. You're free to make it personal and tailor it to your family's needs and preferences. I want you to
know that you *can* meet your kids right where they are, and build them
up to be confident, resilient, and mentally healthy kids who are following
their dreams and passions, along the way to becoming the incredible adults
they're meant to be – no matter what.

You are meeting your kids' needs every day in teeny tiny ways and big,
huge ways, and you need to be encouraged. You need to trust that you can
not only make it homeschooling your kids through high school, but thrive
while doing it. You can enjoy the process of learning alongside your kids,
the rabbit trails followed by not knowing every answer to every question,
and the adventure of discovering wonder through the eyes of your little
ones *and* your teens. And you can do all this in a way that lights up your
unique family, taps into your individual and collective strengths, and leads
you to follow interests and passions.

Silver bullets and magic potions don't exist in the homeschooling world.
The best way to homeschool is highly personal and individual. I once read
through a comment thread on a post a mom had shared in a homeschooling support group on Facebook. This mom had come to the group asking
for book and curriculum recommendations for her six-year-old. It seems
her kiddo was devouring every book she could get her hands on, was asking for more, and wanted her mom to buy her workbooks so she could, in
the child's word, "answer questions about the books" she was reading. That
poor mom was slammed in the comments. Other moms chimed in, chastis-
ing her for *pushing her child*, telling her to *just let her be a kid and play*, and
that the best books for a six-year-old were those read aloud and the best
curriculum was play.

And that is true for most children. I tell parents to buy less than they think they need and play more than they think they should when they ask me about curriculum for young children. But the other advice I give, always be a student of your child, trumps that. What those other moms didn't understand was, to that child and her unique brain, reading challenging books and answering questions about them *was* play. To my now 21-year-old, however, reading books wasn't ever play. It was torture – especially at six.

Kids' brains are wired differently – whether a child is neurodivergent or neurotypical – and they need to be met where they are; their strengths honored, appreciated, and respected; and their interests and passions tapped into. For some, that means a workbook and study guide. For others, that means a walk in the woods with a field guide. For still others, that means documentaries, books, and art projects all on one topic for days and days on end. Some kids struggle. Some excel. Still others struggle in some areas while excelling in different ones.

I know kids – they're amazing and beautiful and clever and creative, each in their own ways.

I know homeschooling parents. Some doubt. Some are confident. Still others vacillate between those feelings and more.

Deepak Chopra once said, "If a child is poor in math but good at tennis, most people would hire a math tutor. I would rather hire a tennis coach." Our schools tend to focus on the deficits, placing kids in remedial classes, giving them more homework for extra practice, and call parents in to talk about the problems, suggest testing, and often, medication. Homeschooling allows us to flip the script and focus on the strengths as Deepak Chopra suggests. We can maximize our kids' interests and the things they're great at, while helping them take the time to learn the tough stuff slowly and master it at their own pace.

When we focus on our kids' strengths, passions, and interests, we build motivation, increase their confidence, and build stronger, mentally healthier kids.

I hope you know what an advantage you are giving your kids and their future by homeschooling them. You are incredible. Have confidence in yourself, remembering that you are the perfect parent for your perfect kiddos **and** you are the absolute best teacher they could ever have. Be brave.

You've got this, friend.

Trust yourself.

Additional Resources

Throughout this book, I've referenced books and websites about the different topics I've covered. This section includes more books and websites you may be interested in, as there are so many incredible resources out there for homeschool families. If you prefer going online to a page that has every resource linked for you to connect to directly, I've created that for you at: https://homeschooladvantage.resources

Books

8 Great Smarts for Home Schoolers, by Kathy Koch and Tina Hollenbeck
A Place to Belong, by Amber O'Neal Johnston
Better Together, by Pam Barnhill
Big Book of Unschooling, by Nancy Wallace
Creative Homeschooling, by Lisa Rivero
Different By Design Learning, by Shawna Wingert
Dumbing Us Down, by John Taylor Gatto
Educating the Wholehearted Child, by Clay Clarkson and Sally Clarkson
Free-Range Kids, by Lenore Skenazy
Free Range Learning, by Laura Grace Weldon
Free to Learn, by Peter Gray Ph.D.

Give Your Child the World, by Jamie C. Martin
Homeschool Bravely, by Jamie Erickson
Homeschool Made Easy, by Lea Ann Garfias
Homeschool Rising, by Christy-Faith
Homeschooling Gifted Kids, by Cindy West
Modern Miss Mason, by Leah Boden
Parenting Beyond the Rules, by Connie Albers
Plan Your Year, by Pam Barnhill
Raising Critical Thinkers, by Julie Bogart
Raising Resilient Sons, by Colleen Kessler
Simplicity Parenting, by Kim John Payne
Teach Your Own, by John Taylor Gatto and Pat Farenga
Teaching from Rest, by Sarah Mackenzie
The 4 Hour School Day, by Durenda Wilson
The Art of Self-Directed Learning, by Blake Boles
The Brave Learner, by Julie Bogart
The Call of the Wild and Free, by Ainsley Arment
The Read Aloud Family, by Sarah Mackenzie
The Self-Driven Child, by Ned Johnson and William Stixrud, Ph.D.
The Teenage Liberation Handbook, by Grace Llewellyn
The Year of Learning Dangerously, by Quinn Cummings
Unschooled, by Kerry McDonald

Websites

Celebrate a Book with Mary Hanna Wilson
www.MaryHannaWilson.com
The author creates fun book parties and hosts online book clubs through Outschool.

Christy-Faith
www.Christy-Faith.com
Resources by a long-time expert in the field of education and homeschool advocate.

Different By Design Learning

www.DifferentByDesignLearning.com

This online hub caters to homeschool children with unique differences through a strength-based, interest-led approach.

Homeschool Advantage

www.HomeschoolAdvantageBook.com

The page for this book with links to resources, a book guide, free printables, and more.

Homeschool Advantage Resources

www.HomeschoolAdvantage.resources

A page with linked, chapter-by-chapter resources.

Homeschool OT

www.HomeschoolOT.com

Occupational therapist turned homeschool mom offers loads of resources for helping neurodivergent kiddos regulate their bodies and teaches parents to help.

Homeschooling Today

www.HomeschoolingToday.com

Founded by two homeschool moms, Homeschooling Today is a resource-rich site and a quarterly print magazine.

Homegrown Learners

www.HomegrownLearners.com

Founded by a former public school teacher and creator of the SQUILT music program, this website is filled with articles, resources, and printables.

Our Journey Westward

www.OurJourneyWestward.com

A treasure trove of project-based learning, unit studies, and our family's favorite nature study program.

Raising Lifelong Learners

www.RaisingLifelongLearners.com

The author's website with resources, articles, and more.

Read Aloud Revival

www.ReadAloudRevival.com

The author of this site believes in connecting through books. It's a rich site with a podcast, booklists, and a vibrant community.

Simple Homeschool

www.SimpleHomeschool.net

Created with the purpose of demonstrating that homeschooling is a lifestyle approach. Written by various contributors (including the author of this book).

Your Morning Basket

www.PamBarnhill.com

Morning time is a time to gather as a family and focus on the good, true, and beautiful. This site offers resources to help with that.

Index